ISBN 0-8373-0171-8

C-171   CAREER EXAMINATION SERIES

This is your
PASSBOOK® for...

Court Clerk

Test Preparation Study Guide

Questions & Answers

NATIONAL LEARNING CORPORATION

PASSBOOK®

NOTICE

This book is SOLELY intended for, is sold ONLY to, and its use is RESTRICTED to *individual*, bona fide applicants or candidates who qualify by virtue of having seriously filed applications for appropriate license, certificate, professional and/or promotional advancement, higher school matriculation, scholarship, or other legitimate requirements of educational and/or governmental authorities.

This book is NOT intended for use, class instruction, tutoring, training, duplication, copying, reprinting, excerption, or adaptation, etc., by:

(1) Other publishers

(2) Proprietors and/or Instructors of "Coaching" and/or Preparatory Courses

(3) Personnel and/or Training Divisions of commercial, industrial, and governmental organizations

(4) Schools, colleges, or universities and/or their departments and staffs, including teachers and other personnel

(5) Testing Agencies or Bureaus

(6) Study groups which seek by the purchase of a single volume to copy and/or duplicate and/or adapt this material for use by the group as a whole without having purchased individual volumes for each of the members of the group

(7) Et al.

Such persons would be in violation of appropriate Federal and State statutes.

PROVISION OF LICENSING AGREEMENTS. — Recognized educational commercial, industrial, and governmental institutions and organizations, and others legitimately engaged in educational pursuits, including training, testing, and measurement activities, may address a request for a licensing agreement to the copyright owners, who will determine whether, and under what conditions, including fees and charges, the materials in this book may be used by them. In other words, a licensing facility exists for the legitimate use of the material in this book on other than an individual basis. However, it is asseverated and affirmed here that the material in this book *CANNOT* be used without the receipt of the express permission of such a licensing agreement from the Publishers.

NATIONAL LEARNING CORPORATION
212 Michael Drive
Syosset, New York 11791

Inquiries re licensing agreements should be addressed to:
The President
National Learning Corporation
212 Michael Drive
Syosset, New York 11791

PASSBOOK SERIES®

THE *PASSBOOK SERIES®* has been created to prepare applicants and candidates for the ultimate academic battlefield – the examination room.

At some time in our lives, each and every one of us may be required to take an examination – for validation, matriculation, admission, qualification, registration, certification, or licensure.

Based on the assumption that every applicant or candidate has met the basic formal educational standards, has taken the required number of courses, and read the necessary texts, the *PASSBOOK SERIES®* furnishes the one special preparation which may assure passing with confidence, instead of failing with insecurity. Examination questions – together with answers – are furnished as the basic vehicle for study so that the mysteries of the examination and its compounding difficulties may be eliminated or diminished by a sure method.

This book is meant to help you pass your examination provided that you qualify and are serious in your objective.

The entire field is reviewed through the huge store of content information which is succinctly presented through a provocative and challenging approach – the question-and-answer method.

A climate of success is established by furnishing the correct answers at the end of each test.

You soon learn to recognize types of questions, forms of questions, and patterns of questioning. You may even begin to anticipate expected outcomes.

You perceive that many questions are repeated or adapted so that you can gain acute insights, which may enable you to score many sure points.

You learn how to confront new questions, or types of questions, and to attack them confidently and work out the correct answers.

You note objectives and emphases, and recognize pitfalls and dangers, so that you may make positive educational adjustments.

Moreover, you are kept fully informed in relation to new concepts, methods, practices, and directions in the field.

You discover that you are actually taking the examination all the time: you are preparing for the examination by "taking" an examination, not by reading extraneous and/or supererogatory textbooks.

In short, this PASSBOOK®, used directedly, should be an important factor in helping you to pass your test.

COURT CLERK

DUTIES
Reviews and processes court documents and proceedings; may supervise subordinate clerical personnel; performs related duties as required.

SUBJECT OF EXAMINATION
The written test will be designed to test for knowledge, skills, and/or abilities in such areas as:
1. Office record keeping;
2. Clerical operations with letters and numbers;
3. Name and number checking; and
4. Understanding and interpreting written material.

HOW TO TAKE A TEST

I. YOU MUST PASS AN EXAMINATION

A. WHAT EVERY CANDIDATE SHOULD KNOW

Examination applicants often ask us for help in preparing for the written test. What can I study in advance? What kinds of questions will be asked? How will the test be given? How will the papers be graded?

As an applicant for a civil service examination, you may be wondering about some of these things. Our purpose here is to suggest effective methods of advance study and to describe civil service examinations.

Your chances for success on this examination can be increased if you know how to prepare. Those "pre-examination jitters" can be reduced if you know what to expect. You can even experience an adventure in good citizenship if you know why civil service exams are given.

B. WHY ARE CIVIL SERVICE EXAMINATIONS GIVEN?

Civil service examinations are important to you in two ways. As a citizen, you want public jobs filled by employees who know how to do their work. As a job seeker, you want a fair chance to compete for that job on an equal footing with other candidates. The best-known means of accomplishing this two-fold goal is the competitive examination.

Exams are widely publicized throughout the nation. They may be administered for jobs in federal, state, city, municipal, town or village governments or agencies.

Any citizen may apply, with some limitations, such as the age or residence of applicants. Your experience and education may be reviewed to see whether you meet the requirements for the particular examination. When these requirements exist, they are reasonable and applied consistently to all applicants. Thus, a competitive examination may cause you some uneasiness now, but it is your privilege and safeguard.

C. HOW ARE CIVIL SERVICE EXAMS DEVELOPED?

Examinations are carefully written by trained technicians who are specialists in the field known as "psychological measurement," in consultation with recognized authorities in the field of work that the test will cover. These experts recommend the subject matter areas or skills to be tested; only those knowledges or skills important to your success on the job are included. The most reliable books and source materials available are used as references. Together, the experts and technicians judge the difficulty level of the questions.

Test technicians know how to phrase questions so that the problem is clearly stated. Their ethics do not permit "trick" or "catch" questions. Questions may have been tried out on sample groups, or subjected to statistical analysis, to determine their usefulness.

Written tests are often used in combination with performance tests, ratings of training and experience, and oral interviews. All of these measures combine to form the best-known means of finding the right person for the right job.

II. HOW TO PASS THE WRITTEN TEST

A. NATURE OF THE EXAMINATION

To prepare intelligently for civil service examinations, you should know how they differ from school examinations you have taken. In school you were assigned certain definite pages to read or subjects to cover. The examination questions were quite detailed and usually emphasized memory. Civil service exams, on the other hand, try to discover your present ability to perform the duties of a position, plus your potentiality to learn these duties. In other words, a civil service exam attempts to predict how successful you will be. Questions cover such a broad area that they cannot be as minute and detailed as school exam questions.

In the public service similar kinds of work, or positions, are grouped together in one "class." This process is known as *position-classification*. All the positions in a class are paid according to the salary range for that class. One class title covers all of these positions, and they are all tested by the same examination.

B. FOUR BASIC STEPS

1) Study the announcement

How, then, can you know what subjects to study? Our best answer is: "Learn as much as possible about the class of positions for which you've applied." The exam will test the knowledge, skills and abilities needed to do the work.

Your most valuable source of information about the position you want is the official exam announcement. This announcement lists the training and experience qualifications. Check these standards and apply only if you come reasonably close to meeting them.

The brief description of the position in the examination announcement offers some clues to the subjects which will be tested. Think about the job itself. Review the duties in your mind. Can you perform them, or are there some in which you are rusty? Fill in the blank spots in your preparation.

Many jurisdictions preview the written test in the exam announcement by including a section called "Knowledge and Abilities Required," "Scope of the Examination," or some similar heading. Here you will find out specifically what fields will be tested.

2) Review your own background

Once you learn in general what the position is all about, and what you need to know to do the work, ask yourself which subjects you already know fairly well and which need improvement. You may wonder whether to concentrate on improving your strong areas or on building some background in your fields of weakness. When the announcement has specified "some knowledge" or "considerable knowledge," or has used adjectives like "beginning principles of…" or "advanced … methods," you can get a clue as to the number and difficulty of questions to be asked in any given field. More questions, and hence broader coverage, would be included for those subjects which are more important in the work. Now weigh your strengths and weaknesses against the job requirements and prepare accordingly.

3) Determine the level of the position

Another way to tell how intensively you should prepare is to understand the level of the job for which you are applying. Is it the entering level? In other words, is this the position in which beginners in a field of work are hired? Or is it an intermediate or advanced level? Sometimes this is indicated by such words as "Junior" or "Senior" in the class title. Other jurisdictions use Roman numerals to designate the level – Clerk I, Clerk II, for example. The word "Supervisor" sometimes appears in the title. If the level is not indicated by the title, check the description of duties. Will you be working under very close supervision, or will you have responsibility for independent decisions in this work?

4) Choose appropriate study materials

Now that you know the subjects to be examined and the relative amount of each subject to be covered, you can choose suitable study materials. For beginning level jobs, or even advanced ones, if you have a pronounced weakness in some aspect of your training, read a modern, standard textbook in that field. Be sure it is up to date and has general coverage. Such books are normally available at your library, and the librarian will be glad to help you locate one. For entry-level positions, questions of appropriate difficulty are chosen – neither highly advanced questions, nor those too simple. Such questions require careful thought but not advanced training.

If the position for which you are applying is technical or advanced, you will read more advanced, specialized material. If you are already familiar with the basic principles of your field, elementary textbooks would waste your time. Concentrate on advanced textbooks and technical periodicals. Think through the concepts and review difficult problems in your field.

These are all general sources. You can get more ideas on your own initiative, following these leads. For example, training manuals and publications of the government agency which employs workers in your field can be useful, particularly for technical and professional positions. A letter or visit to the government department involved may result in more specific study suggestions, and certainly will provide you with a more definite idea of the exact nature of the position you are seeking.

III. KINDS OF TESTS

Tests are used for purposes other than measuring knowledge and ability to perform specified duties. For some positions, it is equally important to test ability to make adjustments to new situations or to profit from training. In others, basic mental abilities not dependent on information are essential. Questions which test these things may not appear as pertinent to the duties of the position as those which test for knowledge and information. Yet they are often highly important parts of a fair examination. For very general questions, it is almost impossible to help you direct your study efforts. What we can do is to point out some of the more common of these general abilities needed in public service positions and describe some typical questions.

1) General information

Broad, general information has been found useful for predicting job success in some kinds of work. This is tested in a variety of ways, from vocabulary lists to questions about current events. Basic background in some field of work, such as sociology or economics, may be sampled in a group of questions. Often these are principles which have become familiar to most persons through exposure rather than through formal training. It is difficult to advise you how to study for these questions; being alert to the world around you is our best suggestion.

2) Verbal ability

An example of an ability needed in many positions is verbal or language ability. Verbal ability is, in brief, the ability to use and understand words. Vocabulary and grammar tests are typical measures of this ability. Reading comprehension or paragraph interpretation questions are common in many kinds of civil service tests. You are given a paragraph of written material and asked to find its central meaning.

3) Numerical ability

Number skills can be tested by the familiar arithmetic problem, by checking paired lists of numbers to see which are alike and which are different, or by interpreting charts and graphs. In the latter test, a graph may be printed in the test booklet which you are asked to use as the basis for answering questions.

4) Observation

A popular test for law-enforcement positions is the observation test. A picture is shown to you for several minutes, then taken away. Questions about the picture test your ability to observe both details and larger elements.

5) Following directions

In many positions in the public service, the employee must be able to carry out written instructions dependably and accurately. You may be given a chart with several columns, each column listing a variety of information. The questions require you to carry out directions involving the information given in the chart.

6) Skills and aptitudes

Performance tests effectively measure some manual skills and aptitudes. When the skill is one in which you are trained, such as typing or shorthand, you can practice. These tests are often very much like those given in business school or high school courses. For many of the other skills and aptitudes, however, no short-time preparation can be made. Skills and abilities natural to you or that you have developed throughout your lifetime are being tested.

Many of the general questions just described provide all the data needed to answer the questions and ask you to use your reasoning ability to find the answers. Your best preparation for these tests, as well as for tests of facts and ideas, is to be at your physical and mental best. You, no doubt, have your own methods of getting into an exam-taking mood and keeping "in shape." The next section lists some ideas on this subject.

IV. KINDS OF QUESTIONS

Only rarely is the "essay" question, which you answer in narrative form, used in civil service tests. Civil service tests are usually of the short-answer type. Full instructions for answering these questions will be given to you at the examination. But in case this is your first experience with short-answer questions and separate answer sheets, here is what you need to know:

4

1) Multiple-choice Questions

Most popular of the short-answer questions is the "multiple choice" or "best answer" question. It can be used, for example, to test for factual knowledge, ability to solve problems or judgment in meeting situations found at work.

A multiple-choice question is normally one of three types—

- It can begin with an incomplete statement followed by several possible endings. You are to find the one ending which *best* completes the statement, although some of the others may not be entirely wrong.
- It can also be a complete statement in the form of a question which is answered by choosing one of the statements listed.
- It can be in the form of a problem – again you select the best answer.

Here is an example of a multiple-choice question with a discussion which should give you some clues as to the method for choosing the right answer:

When an employee has a complaint about his assignment, the action which will *best* help him overcome his difficulty is to
    A. discuss his difficulty with his coworkers
    B. take the problem to the head of the organization
    C. take the problem to the person who gave him the assignment
    D. say nothing to anyone about his complaint

In answering this question, you should study each of the choices to find which is best. Consider choice "A" – Certainly an employee may discuss his complaint with fellow employees, but no change or improvement can result, and the complaint remains unresolved. Choice "B" is a poor choice since the head of the organization probably does not know what assignment you have been given, and taking your problem to him is known as "going over the head" of the supervisor. The supervisor, or person who made the assignment, is the person who can clarify it or correct any injustice. Choice "C" is, therefore, correct. To say nothing, as in choice "D," is unwise. Supervisors have and interest in knowing the problems employees are facing, and the employee is seeking a solution to his problem.

2) True/False Questions

The "true/false" or "right/wrong" form of question is sometimes used. Here a complete statement is given. Your job is to decide whether the statement is right or wrong.

SAMPLE: A person-to-person long-distance telephone call costs less than a station-to-station call to the same city.

This statement is wrong, or false, since person-to-person calls are more expensive.

This is not a complete list of all possible question forms, although most of the others are variations of these common types. You will always get complete directions for answering questions. Be sure you understand *how* to mark your answers – ask questions until you do.

V. RECORDING YOUR ANSWERS

For an examination with very few applicants, you may be told to record your answers in the test booklet itself. Separate answer sheets are much more common. If this separate answer sheet is to be scored by machine – and this is often the case – it is highly important that you mark your answers correctly in order to get credit.

An electric scoring machine is often used in civil service offices because of the speed with which papers can be scored. Machine-scored answer sheets must be marked with a pencil, which will be given to you. This pencil has a high graphite content which responds to the electric scoring machine. As a matter of fact, stray dots may register as answers, so do not let your pencil rest on the answer sheet while you are pondering the correct answer. Also, if your pencil lead breaks or is otherwise defective, ask for another.

Since the answer sheet will be dropped in a slot in the scoring machine, be careful not to bend the corners or get the paper crumpled.

The answer sheet normally has five vertical columns of numbers, with 30 numbers to a column. These numbers correspond to the question numbers in your test booklet. After each number, going across the page are four or five pairs of dotted lines. These short dotted lines have small letters or numbers above them. The first two pairs may also have a "T" or "F" above the letters. This indicates that the first two pairs only are to be used if the questions are of the true-false type. If the questions are multiple choice, disregard the "T" and "F" and pay attention only to the small letters or numbers.

Answer your questions in the manner of the sample that follows:

    32. The largest city in the United States is
        A. Washington, D.C.
        B. New York City
        C. Chicago
        D. Detroit
        E. San Francisco

1) Choose the answer you think is best. (New York City is the largest, so "B" is correct.)
2) Find the row of dotted lines numbered the same as the question you are answering. (Find row number 32)
3) Find the pair of dotted lines corresponding to the answer. (Find the pair of lines under the mark "B.")
4) Make a solid black mark between the dotted lines.

VI. BEFORE THE TEST

Common sense will help you find procedures to follow to get ready for an examination. Too many of us, however, overlook these sensible measures. Indeed, nervousness and fatigue have been found to be the most serious reasons why applicants fail to do their best on civil service tests. Here is a list of reminders:

- Begin your preparation early – Don't wait until the last minute to go scurrying around for books and materials or to find out what the position is all about.
- Prepare continuously – An hour a night for a week is better than an all-night cram session. This has been definitely established. What is more, a night a

week for a month will return better dividends than crowding your study into a shorter period of time.

- Locate the place of the exam – You have been sent a notice telling you when and where to report for the examination. If the location is in a different town or otherwise unfamiliar to you, it would be well to inquire the best route and learn something about the building.
- Relax the night before the test – Allow your mind to rest. Do not study at all that night. Plan some mild recreation or diversion; then go to bed early and get a good night's sleep.
- Get up early enough to make a leisurely trip to the place for the test – This way unforeseen events, traffic snarls, unfamiliar buildings, etc. will not upset you.
- Dress comfortably – A written test is not a fashion show. You will be known by number and not by name, so wear something comfortable.
- Leave excess paraphernalia at home – Shopping bags and odd bundles will get in your way. You need bring only the items mentioned in the official notice you received; usually everything you need is provided. Do not bring reference books to the exam. They will only confuse those last minutes and be taken away from you when in the test room.
- Arrive somewhat ahead of time – If because of transportation schedules you must get there very early, bring a newspaper or magazine to take your mind off yourself while waiting.
- Locate the examination room – When you have found the proper room, you will be directed to the seat or part of the room where you will sit. Sometimes you are given a sheet of instructions to read while you are waiting. Do not fill out any forms until you are told to do so; just read them and be prepared.
- Relax and prepare to listen to the instructions
- If you have any physical problem that may keep you from doing your best, be sure to tell the test administrator. If you are sick or in poor health, you really cannot do your best on the exam. You can come back and take the test some other time.

VII. AT THE TEST

The day of the test is here and you have the test booklet in your hand. The temptation to get going is very strong. Caution! There is more to success than knowing the right answers. You must know how to identify your papers and understand variations in the type of short-answer question used in this particular examination. Follow these suggestions for maximum results from your efforts:

1) Cooperate with the monitor
The test administrator has a duty to create a situation in which you can be as much at ease as possible. He will give instructions, tell you when to begin, check to see that you are marking your answer sheet correctly, and so on. He is not there to guard you, although he will see that your competitors do not take unfair advantage. He wants to help you do your best.

2) Listen to all instructions
Don't jump the gun! Wait until you understand all directions. In most civil service tests you get more time than you need to answer the questions. So don't be in a hurry.

Read each word of instructions until you clearly understand the meaning. Study the examples, listen to all announcements and follow directions. Ask questions if you do not understand what to do.

3) Identify your papers

Civil service exams are usually identified by number only. You will be assigned a number; you must not put your name on your test papers. Be sure to copy your number correctly. Since more than one exam may be given, copy your exact examination title.

4) Plan your time

Unless you are told that a test is a "speed" or "rate of work" test, speed itself is usually not important. Time enough to answer all the questions will be provided, but this does not mean that you have all day. An overall time limit has been set. Divide the total time (in minutes) by the number of questions to determine the approximate time you have for each question.

5) Do not linger over difficult questions

If you come across a difficult question, mark it with a paper clip (useful to have along) and come back to it when you have been through the booklet. One caution if you do this – be sure to skip a number on your answer sheet as well. Check often to be sure that you have not lost your place and that you are marking in the row numbered the same as the question you are answering.

6) Read the questions

Be sure you know what the question asks! Many capable people are unsuccessful because they failed to *read* the questions correctly.

7) Answer all questions

Unless you have been instructed that a penalty will be deducted for incorrect answers, it is better to guess than to omit a question.

8) Speed tests

It is often better NOT to guess on speed tests. It has been found that on timed tests people are tempted to spend the last few seconds before time is called in marking answers at random – without even reading them – in the hope of picking up a few extra points. To discourage this practice, the instructions may warn you that your score will be "corrected" for guessing. That is, a penalty will be applied. The incorrect answers will be deducted from the correct ones, or some other penalty formula will be used.

9) Review your answers

If you finish before time is called, go back to the questions you guessed or omitted to give them further thought. Review other answers if you have time.

10) Return your test materials

If you are ready to leave before others have finished or time is called, take ALL your materials to the monitor and leave quietly. Never take any test material with you. The monitor can discover whose papers are not complete, and taking a test booklet may be grounds for disqualification.

VIII. EXAMINATION TECHNIQUES

1) Read the general instructions carefully. These are usually printed on the first page of the exam booklet. As a rule, these instructions refer to the timing of the examination; the fact that you should not start work until the signal and must stop work at a signal, etc. If there are any *special* instructions, such as a choice of questions to be answered, make sure that you note this instruction carefully.

2) When you are ready to start work on the examination, that is as soon as the signal has been given, read the instructions to each question booklet, underline any key words or phrases, such as *least, best, outline, describe* and the like. In this way you will tend to answer as requested rather than discover on reviewing your paper that you *listed without describing*, that you selected the *worst* choice rather than the *best* choice, etc.

3) If the examination is of the objective or multiple-choice type – that is, each question will also give a series of possible answers: A, B, C or D, and you are called upon to select the best answer and write the letter next to that answer on your answer paper – it is advisable to start answering each question in turn. There may be anywhere from 50 to 100 such questions in the three or four hours allotted and you can see how much time would be taken if you read through all the questions before beginning to answer any. Furthermore, if you come across a question or group of questions which you know would be difficult to answer, it would undoubtedly affect your handling of all the other questions.

4) If the examination is of the essay type and contains but a few questions, it is a moot point as to whether you should read all the questions before starting to answer any one. Of course, if you are given a choice – say five out of seven and the like – then it is essential to read all the questions so you can eliminate the two that are most difficult. If, however, you are asked to answer all the questions, there may be danger in trying to answer the easiest one first because you may find that you will spend too much time on it. The best technique is to answer the first question, then proceed to the second, etc.

5) Time your answers. Before the exam begins, write down the time it started, then add the time allowed for the examination and write down the time it must be completed, then divide the time available somewhat as follows:
   * If 3-1/2 hours are allowed, that would be 210 minutes. If you have 80 objective-type questions, that would be an average of 2-1/2 minutes per question. Allow yourself no more than 2 minutes per question, or a total of 160 minutes, which will permit about 50 minutes to review.
   * If for the time allotment of 210 minutes there are 7 essay questions to answer, that would average about 30 minutes a question. Give yourself only 25 minutes per question so that you have about 35 minutes to review.

6) The most important instruction is to *read each question* and make sure you know what is wanted. The second most important instruction is to *time yourself properly* so that you answer every question. The third most

important instruction is to *answer every question.* Guess if you have to but include something for each question. Remember that you will receive no credit for a blank and will probably receive some credit if you write something in answer to an essay question. If you guess a letter – say "B" for a multiple-choice question – you may have guessed right. If you leave a blank as an answer to a multiple-choice question, the examiners may respect your feelings but it will not add a point to your score. Some exams may penalize you for wrong answers, so in such cases *only,* you may not want to guess unless you have some basis for your answer.

7) Suggestions
  a. Objective-type questions
    1. Examine the question booklet for proper sequence of pages and questions
    2. Read all instructions carefully
    3. Skip any question which seems too difficult; return to it after all other questions have been answered
    4. Apportion your time properly; do not spend too much time on any single question or group of questions
    5. Note and underline key words – *all, most, fewest, least, best, worst, same, opposite,* etc.
    6. Pay particular attention to negatives
    7. Note unusual option, e.g., unduly long, short, complex, different or similar in content to the body of the question
    8. Observe the use of "hedging" words – *probably, may, most likely,* etc.
    9. Make sure that your answer is put next to the same number as the question
    10. Do not second-guess unless you have good reason to believe the second answer is definitely more correct
    11. Cross out original answer if you decide another answer is more accurate; do not erase until you are ready to hand your paper in
    12. Answer all questions; guess unless instructed otherwise
    13. Leave time for review

  b. Essay questions
    1. Read each question carefully
    2. Determine exactly what is wanted. Underline key words or phrases.
    3. Decide on outline or paragraph answer
    4. Include many different points and elements unless asked to develop any one or two points or elements
    5. Show impartiality by giving pros and cons unless directed to select one side only
    6. Make and write down any assumptions you find necessary to answer the questions
    7. Watch your English, grammar, punctuation and choice of words
    8. Time your answers; don't crowd material

8) Answering the essay question

Most essay questions can be answered by framing the specific response around several key words or ideas. Here are a few such key words or ideas:

M's: manpower, materials, methods, money, management
P's: purpose, program, policy, plan, procedure, practice, problems, pitfalls, personnel, public relations

   a. Six basic steps in handling problems:
1. Preliminary plan and background development
2. Collect information, data and facts
3. Analyze and interpret information, data and facts
4. Analyze and develop solutions as well as make recommendations
5. Prepare report and sell recommendations
6. Install recommendations and follow up effectiveness

   b. Pitfalls to avoid
1. *Taking things for granted* – A statement of the situation does not necessarily imply that each of the elements is necessarily true; for example, a complaint may be invalid and biased so that all that can be taken for granted is that a complaint has been registered
2. *Considering only one side of a situation* – Wherever possible, indicate several alternatives and then point out the reasons you selected the best one
3. *Failing to indicate follow up* – Whenever your answer indicates action on your part, make certain that you will take proper follow-up action to see how successful your recommendations, procedures or actions turn out to be
4. *Taking too long in answering any single question* – Remember to time your answers properly

IX. AFTER THE TEST

Scoring procedures differ in detail among civil service jurisdictions although the general principles are the same. Whether the papers are hand-scored or graded by machine we have described, they are nearly always graded by number. That is, the person who marks the paper knows only the number – never the name – of the applicant. Not until all the papers have been graded will they be matched with names. If other tests, such as training and experience or oral interview ratings have been given, scores will be combined. Different parts of the examination usually have different weights. For example, the written test might count 60 percent of the final grade, and a rating of training and experience 40 percent. In many jurisdictions, veterans will have a certain number of points added to their grades.

After the final grade has been determined, the names are placed in grade order and an eligible list is established. There are various methods for resolving ties between those who get the same final grade – probably the most common is to place first the name of the person whose application was received first. Job offers are made from the eligible list in the order the names appear on it. You will be notified of your grade and your rank as soon as all these computations have been made. This will be done as rapidly as possible.

People who are found to meet the requirements in the announcement are called "eligibles." Their names are put on a list of eligible candidates. An eligible's chances of getting a job depend on how high he stands on this list and how fast agencies are filling jobs from the list.

When a job is to be filled from a list of eligibles, the agency asks for the names of people on the list of eligibles for that job. When the civil service commission receives this request, it sends to the agency the names of the three people highest on this list. Or, if the job to be filled has specialized requirements, the office sends the agency the names of the top three persons who meet these requirements from the general list.

The appointing officer makes a choice from among the three people whose names were sent to him. If the selected person accepts the appointment, the names of the others are put back on the list to be considered for future openings.

That is the rule in hiring from all kinds of eligible lists, whether they are for typist, carpenter, chemist, or something else. For every vacancy, the appointing officer has his choice of any one of the top three eligibles on the list. This explains why the person whose name is on top of the list sometimes does not get an appointment when some of the persons lower on the list do. If the appointing officer chooses the second or third eligible, the No. 1 eligible does not get a job at once, but stays on the list until he is appointed or the list is terminated.

X. HOW TO PASS THE INTERVIEW TEST

The examination for which you applied requires an oral interview test. You have already taken the written test and you are now being called for the interview test – the final part of the formal examination.

You may think that it is not possible to prepare for an interview test and that there are no procedures to follow during an interview. Our purpose is to point out some things you can do in advance that will help you and some good rules to follow and pitfalls to avoid while you are being interviewed.

What is an interview supposed to test?

The written examination is designed to test the technical knowledge and competence of the candidate; the oral is designed to evaluate intangible qualities, not readily measured otherwise, and to establish a list showing the relative fitness of each candidate – as measured against his competitors – for the position sought. Scoring is not on the basis of "right" and "wrong," but on a sliding scale of values ranging from "not passable" to "outstanding." As a matter of fact, it is possible to achieve a relatively low score without a single "incorrect" answer because of evident weakness in the qualities being measured.

Occasionally, an examination may consist entirely of an oral test – either an individual or a group oral. In such cases, information is sought concerning the technical knowledges and abilities of the candidate, since there has been no written examination for this purpose. More commonly, however, an oral test is used to supplement a written examination.

Who conducts interviews?

The composition of oral boards varies among different jurisdictions. In nearly all, a representative of the personnel department serves as chairman. One of the members of the board may be a representative of the department in which the candidate would work. In some cases, "outside experts" are used, and, frequently, a businessman or some other representative of the general public is asked to serve. Labor and management or other special groups may be represented. The aim is to secure the services of experts in the appropriate field.

However the board is composed, it is a good idea (and not at all improper or unethical) to ascertain in advance of the interview who the members are and what groups they represent. When you are introduced to them, you will have some idea of their backgrounds and interests, and at least you will not stutter and stammer over their names.

What should be done before the interview?

While knowledge about the board members is useful and takes some of the surprise element out of the interview, there is other preparation which is more substantive. It *is* possible to prepare for an oral interview – in several ways:

1) Keep a copy of your application and review it carefully before the interview

This may be the only document before the oral board, and the starting point of the interview. Know what education and experience you have listed there, and the sequence and dates of all of it. Sometimes the board will ask you to review the highlights of your experience for them; you should not have to hem and haw doing it.

2) Study the class specification and the examination announcement

Usually, the oral board has one or both of these to guide them. The qualities, characteristics or knowledges required by the position sought are stated in these documents. They offer valuable clues as to the nature of the oral interview. For example, if the job involves supervisory responsibilities, the announcement will usually indicate that knowledge of modern supervisory methods and the qualifications of the candidate as a supervisor will be tested. If so, you can expect such questions, frequently in the form of a hypothetical situation which you are expected to solve. NEVER go into an oral without knowledge of the duties and responsibilities of the job you seek.

3) Think through each qualification required

Try to visualize the kind of questions you would ask if you were a board member. How well could you answer them? Try especially to appraise your own knowledge and background in each area, *measured against the job sought*, and identify any areas in which you are weak. Be critical and realistic – do not flatter yourself.

4) Do some general reading in areas in which you feel you may be weak

For example, if the job involves supervision and your past experience has NOT, some general reading in supervisory methods and practices, particularly in the field of human relations, might be useful. Do NOT study agency procedures or detailed manuals. The oral board will be testing your understanding and capacity, not your memory.

5) Get a good night's sleep and watch your general health and mental attitude

You will want a clear head at the interview. Take care of a cold or any other minor ailment, and of course, no hangovers.

What should be done on the day of the interview?

Now comes the day of the interview itself. Give yourself plenty of time to get there. Plan to arrive somewhat ahead of the scheduled time, particularly if your appointment is in the fore part of the day. If a previous candidate fails to appear, the board might be ready for you a bit early. By early afternoon an oral board is almost invariably behind schedule if there are many candidates, and you may have to wait.

Take along a book or magazine to read, or your application to review, but leave any extraneous material in the waiting room when you go in for your interview. In any event, relax and compose yourself.

The matter of dress is important. The board is forming impressions about you – from your experience, your manners, your attitude, and your appearance. Give your personal appearance careful attention. Dress your best, but not your flashiest. Choose conservative, appropriate clothing, and be sure it is immaculate. This is a business interview, and your appearance should indicate that you regard it as such. Besides, being well groomed and properly dressed will help boost your confidence.

Sooner or later, someone will call your name and escort you into the interview room. *This is it.* From here on you are on your own. It is too late for any more preparation. But remember, you asked for this opportunity to prove your fitness, and you are here because your request was granted.

What happens when you go in?

The usual sequence of events will be as follows: The clerk (who is often the board stenographer) will introduce you to the chairman of the oral board, who will introduce you to the other members of the board. Acknowledge the introductions before you sit down. Do not be surprised if you find a microphone facing you or a stenotypist sitting by. Oral interviews are usually recorded in the event of an appeal or other review.

Usually the chairman of the board will open the interview by reviewing the highlights of your education and work experience from your application – primarily for the benefit of the other members of the board, as well as to get the material into the record. Do not interrupt or comment unless there is an error or significant misinterpretation; if that is the case, do not hesitate. But do not quibble about insignificant matters. Also, he will usually ask you some question about your education, experience or your present job – partly to get you to start talking and to establish the interviewing "rapport." He may start the actual questioning, or turn it over to one of the other members. Frequently, each member undertakes the questioning on a particular area, one in which he is perhaps most competent, so you can expect each member to participate in the examination. Because time is limited, you may also expect some rather abrupt switches in the direction the questioning takes, so do not be upset by it. Normally, a board member will not pursue a single line of questioning unless he discovers a particular strength or weakness.

After each member has participated, the chairman will usually ask whether any member has any further questions, then will ask you if you have anything you wish to add. Unless you are expecting this question, it may floor you. Worse, it may start you off on an extended, extemporaneous speech. The board is not usually seeking more information. The question is principally to offer you a last opportunity to present further qualifications or to indicate that you have nothing to add. So, if you feel that a significant qualification or characteristic has been overlooked, it is proper to point it out in a sentence or so. Do not compliment the board on the thoroughness of their examination – they have been sketchy, and you know it. If you wish, merely say, "No thank you, I have nothing further to add." This is a point where you can "talk yourself out" of a good impression or fail to present an important bit of information. Remember, *you close the interview yourself.*

The chairman will then say, "That is all, Mr. _____, thank you." Do not be startled; the interview is over, and quicker than you think. Thank him, gather your belongings and take your leave. Save your sigh of relief for the other side of the door.

How to put your best foot forward

Throughout this entire process, you may feel that the board individually and collectively is trying to pierce your defenses, seek out your hidden weaknesses and embarrass and confuse you. Actually, this is not true. They are obliged to make an appraisal of your qualifications for the job you are seeking, and they want to see you in your best light. Remember, they must interview all candidates and a non-cooperative candidate may become a failure in spite of their best efforts to bring out his qualifications. Here are 15 suggestions that will help you:

1) Be natural – Keep your attitude confident, not cocky

If you are not confident that you can do the job, do not expect the board to be. Do not apologize for your weaknesses, try to bring out your strong points. The board is interested in a positive, not negative, presentation. Cockiness will antagonize any board member and make him wonder if you are covering up a weakness by a false show of strength.

2) Get comfortable, but don't lounge or sprawl

Sit erectly but not stiffly. A careless posture may lead the board to conclude that you are careless in other things, or at least that you are not impressed by the importance of the occasion. Either conclusion is natural, even if incorrect. Do not fuss with your clothing, a pencil or an ashtray. Your hands may occasionally be useful to emphasize a point; do not let them become a point of distraction.

3) Do not wisecrack or make small talk

This is a serious situation, and your attitude should show that you consider it as such. Further, the time of the board is limited – they do not want to waste it, and neither should you.

4) Do not exaggerate your experience or abilities

In the first place, from information in the application or other interviews and sources, the board may know more about you than you think. Secondly, you probably will not get away with it. An experienced board is rather adept at spotting such a situation, so do not take the chance.

5) If you know a board member, do not make a point of it, yet do not hide it

Certainly you are not fooling him, and probably not the other members of the board. Do not try to take advantage of your acquaintanceship – it will probably do you little good.

6) Do not dominate the interview

Let the board do that. They will give you the clues – do not assume that you have to do all the talking. Realize that the board has a number of questions to ask you, and do not try to take up all the interview time by showing off your extensive knowledge of the answer to the first one.

7) Be attentive

You only have 20 minutes or so, and you should keep your attention at its sharpest throughout. When a member is addressing a problem or question to you, give him your undivided attention. Address your reply principally to him, but do not exclude the other board members.

8) Do not interrupt

A board member may be stating a problem for you to analyze. He will ask you a question when the time comes. Let him state the problem, and wait for the question.

9) Make sure you understand the question

Do not try to answer until you are sure what the question is. If it is not clear, restate it in your own words or ask the board member to clarify it for you. However, do not haggle about minor elements.

10) Reply promptly but not hastily

A common entry on oral board rating sheets is "candidate responded readily," or "candidate hesitated in replies." Respond as promptly and quickly as you can, but do not jump to a hasty, ill-considered answer.

11) Do not be peremptory in your answers

A brief answer is proper – but do not fire your answer back. That is a losing game from your point of view. The board member can probably ask questions much faster than you can answer them.

12) Do not try to create the answer you think the board member wants

He is interested in what kind of mind you have and how it works – not in playing games. Furthermore, he can usually spot this practice and will actually grade you down on it.

13) Do not switch sides in your reply merely to agree with a board member

Frequently, a member will take a contrary position merely to draw you out and to see if you are willing and able to defend your point of view. Do not start a debate, yet do not surrender a good position. If a position is worth taking, it is worth defending.

14) Do not be afraid to admit an error in judgment if you are shown to be wrong

The board knows that you are forced to reply without any opportunity for careful consideration. Your answer may be demonstrably wrong. If so, admit it and get on with the interview.

15) Do not dwell at length on your present job

The opening question may relate to your present assignment. Answer the question but do not go into an extended discussion. You are being examined for a *new* job, not your present one. As a matter of fact, try to phrase ALL your answers in terms of the job for which you are being examined.

Basis of Rating

Probably you will forget most of these "do's" and "don'ts" when you walk into the oral interview room. Even remembering them all will not ensure you a passing grade. Perhaps you did not have the qualifications in the first place. But remembering them will help you to put your best foot forward, without treading on the toes of the board members.

Rumor and popular opinion to the contrary notwithstanding, an oral board wants you to make the best appearance possible. They know you are under pressure – but they also want to see how you respond to it as a guide to what your reaction would be under the pressures of the job you seek. They will be influenced by the degree of poise you display, the personal traits you show and the manner in which you respond.

EXAMINATION SECTION

EXAMINATION SECTION
TEST 1

DIRECTIONS: Each question or incomplete statement is followed by several suggested answers or completions. Select the one that BEST answers the question or completes the statement. *PRINT THE LETTER OF THE CORRECT ANSWER IN THE SPACE AT THE RIGHT.*

Questions 1-9.

DIRECTIONS: Questions 1 through 9 consist of sentences which may or may not be examples of good English usage. Consider grammar, punctuation, spelling, capitalization, awkwardness, etc. Examine each sentence, and then choose the correct statement about it from the four choices below it. If the English usage in the sentence given is better than it would be with any of the changes suggested in options B, C, and D, choose option A. Do not choose an option that will change the meaning of the sentence.

1. According to Judge Frank, the grocer's sons found guilty of assault and sentenced last Thursday.   1.____

    A. This is an example of acceptable writing.
    B. A comma should be placed after the word *sentenced.*
    C. The word *were* should be placed after *sons*
    D. The apostrophe in *grocer's* should be placed after the *s.*

2. The department heads assistant said that the stenographers should type duplicate copies of all contracts, leases, and bills.   2.____

    A. This is an example of acceptable writing.
    B. A comma should be placed before the word *contracts.*
    C. An apostrophe should be placed before the *s* in *heads.*
    D. Quotation marks should be placed before *the stenographers* and after *bills.*

3. The lawyers questioned the men to determine who was the true property owner?   3.____

    A. This is an example of acceptable writing.
    B. The phrase *questioned the men* should be changed to *asked the men questions.*
    C. The word *was* should be changed to *were.*
    D. The question mark should be changed to a period.

4. The terms stated in the present contract are more specific than those stated in the previous contract.   4.____

    A. This is an example of acceptable writing.
    B. The word *are* should be changed to *is.*
    C. The word *than* should be changed to *then.*
    D. The word *specific* should be changed to *specified.*

5. Of the lawyers considered, the one who argued more skillful was chosen for the job.   5.____

    A. This is an example of acceptable writing.
    B. The word *more* should be replaced by the word *most.*
    C. The word *skillful* should be replaced by the word *skillfully,*
    D. The word *chosen* should be replaced by the word *selected.*

6. Each of the states has a court of appeals; some states have circuit courts.

    A. This is an example of acceptable writing.
    B. The semi-colon should be changed to a comma.
    C. The word *has* should be changed to *have*.
    D. The word *some* should be capitalized.

7. The court trial has greatly effected the child's mental condition.

    A. This is an example of acceptable writing.
    B. The word *effected* should be changed to *affected*.
    C. The word *greatly* should be placed after *effected*.
    D. The apostrophe in *child's* should be placed after the *s*.

8. Last week, the petition signed by all the officers was sent to the Better Business Bureau.

    A. This is an example of acceptable writing.
    B. The phrase *last week* should be placed after *officers*.
    C. A comma should be placed after *petition*.
    D. The word *was* should be changed to *were*.

9. Mr. Farrell claims that he requested form A-12, and three booklets describing court procedures.

    A. This is an example of acceptable writing.
    B. The word *that* should be eliminated.
    C. A colon should be placed after *requested*.
    D. The comma after *A-12* should be eliminated.

Questions 10-21.

DIRECTIONS: Questions 10 through 21 contain a word in capital letters followed by four suggested meanings of the word. For each question, choose the BEST meaning for the word in capital letters.

10. SIGNATORY - A

    A. lawyer who draws up a legal document
    B. document that must be signed by a judge
    C. person who signs a document
    D. true copy of a signature

11. RETAINER - A

    A. fee paid to a lawyer for his services
    B. document held by a third party
    C. court decision to send a prisoner back to custody pending trial
    D. legal requirement to keep certain types of files

12. BEQUEATH - To

    A. receive assistance from a charitable organization
    B. give personal property by will to another
    C. transfer real property from one person to another
    D. receive an inheritance upon the death of a relative

13. RATIFY - To 13.____

    A. approve and sanction   B. forego
    C. produce evidence   D. summarize

14. CODICIL - A 14.____

    A. document introduced in evidence in a civil action
    B. subsection of a law
    C. type of legal action that can be brought by a plaintiff
    D. supplement or an addition to a will

15. ALIAS 15.____

    A. Assumed name   B. In favor of
    C. Against   D. A writ

16. PROXY - A(n) 16.____

    A. phony document in a real estate transaction
    B. opinion by a judge of a civil court
    C. document containing appointment of an agent
    D. summons in a lawsuit

17. ALLEGED 17.____

    A. Innocent   B. Asserted
    C. Guilty   D. Called upon

18. EXECUTE - To 18.____

    A. complete a legal document by signing it
    B. set requirements
    C. render services to a duly elected executive of a municipality
    D. initiate legal action such as a lawsuit

19. NOTARY PUBLIC - A 19.____

    A. lawyer who is running for public office
    B. judge who hears minor cases
    C. public officer, one of whose functions is to administer oaths
    D. lawyer who gives free legal services to persons unable to pay

20. WAIVE - To 20.____

    A. disturb a calm state of affairs
    B. knowingly renounce a right or claim
    C. pardon someone for a minor fault
    D. purposely mislead a person during an investigation

21. ARRAIGN - To 21.____

    A. prevent an escape   B. defend a prisoner
    C. verify a document   D. accuse in a court of law

Questions 22-40.

DIRECTIONS: Questions 22 through 40 each consist of four words which may or may not be spelled correctly. If you find an error in
only one word, mark your answer A;
any two words, mark your answer B;
any three words, mark your answer C;
none of these words, mark your answer D.

22.	occurrence	Febuary	privilege	similiar
23.	separate	transferring	analyze	column
24.	develop	license	bankrupcy	abreviate
25.	subpoena	arguement	dissolution	foreclosure
26.	exaggerate	fundamental	significance	warrant
27.	citizen	endorsed	marraige	appraissal
28.	precedant	univercity	observence	preliminary
29.	stipulate	negligence	judgment	prominent
30.	judisial	whereas	release	guardian
31.	appeal	larcenny	transcrip	jurist
32.	petition	tenancy	agenda	insurance
33.	superfical	premise	morgaged	maintainance
34.	testamony	publically	installment	possessed
35.	escrow	decree	eviction	miscelaneous
36.	securitys	abeyance	adhere	corporate
37.	kaleidoscope	anesthesia	vermilion	tafetta
38.	congruant	barrenness	plebescite	vigilance
39.	picnicing	promisory	resevoir	omission
40.	supersede	banister	wholly	seize

KEY (CORRECT ANSWERS)

1.	C	11.	A	21.	D	31.	B
2.	C	12.	B	22.	B	32.	D
3.	D	13.	A	23.	D	33.	C
4.	A	14.	D	24.	B	34.	B
5.	C	15.	A	25.	A	35.	A
6.	A	16.	C	26.	D	36.	A
7.	B	17.	B	27.	B	37.	A
8.	A	18.	A	28.	C	38.	B
9.	D	19.	C	29.	D	39.	C
10.	C	20.	B	30.	A	40.	D

EXAMINATION SECTION
TEST 1

DIRECTIONS: Each question or incomplete statement is followed by several suggested answers or completions. Select the one that BEST answers the question or completes the statement. *PRINT THE LETTER OF THE CORRECT ANSWER IN THE SPACE AT THE RIGHT.*

Questions 1-6.

DIRECTIONS: Questions 1 through 6 consist of descriptions of material to which a filing designation must be assigned.

Assume that the matters and oases described in the questions were referred for handling to a government legal office which has its files set up according to these file designations. The file designation consists of a number of characters and punctuation marks as described below.

The first character refers to agencies whose legal work is handled by this office. These agencies are numbered consecutively in the order in which they first submit a matter for attention, and are identified in an alphabetical card index. To date numbers have been assigned to agencies as follows:

Department of Correction	*1*
Police Department	*2*
Department of Traffic	*3*
Department of Consumer Affairs	*4*
Commission on Human Rights	*5*
Board of Elections	*6*
Department of Personnel	*7*
Board of Estimate	*8*

The second character is separated from the first character by a dash. The second character is the last digit of the year in which a particular lawsuit or matter is referred to the legal office.

The third character is separated from the second character by a colon and may consist of either of the following:

I. *A sub-number assigned to each lawsuit to which the agency is a party. Lawsuits are numbered consecutively regardless of year. (Lawsuits are brought by or against agency heads rather than agencies themselves, but references are made to agencies for the purpose of simplification.)*

or II. *A capital letter assigned to each matter other than a lawsuit according to subject, the subject being identified in an alphabetical index. To date, letters have been assigned to subjects as follows:*

Citizenship	*A*	*Housing*	*E*
Discrimination	*B*	*Gambling*	*F*
Residence Requirements	*C*	*Freedom of Religion*	*G*
Civil Service Examinations	*D*		

These referrals are numbered consecutively regardless of year. The first referral by a particular agency on citizenship, for example, would be designated A1, followed by A2, A3, etc.

If no reference is made in a question as to how many letters involving a certain subject or how much lawsuits have been referred by an agency, assume that it is the first.

For each question, choose the file designation which is MOST appropriate for filing the material described in the question.

1. In January, 2000, two candidates in a 1999 civil service examination for positions with the Department of Correction filed a suit against the Department of Personnel seeking to set aside an educational requirement for the title.
    The Department of Personnel immediately referred the law-suit to the legal office for handling.

    A. 1-9:1   B. 1-0:D1   C. 7-9:D1   D. 7-0:1

2. In 2004, the Police Department made its sixth request for an opinion on whether an employee assignment proposed for 2005 could be considered discriminatory.

    A. 2-5:1-B6   B. 2-4:6   C. 2-4:1-B6   D. 2-4:B6

3. In 2005, a lawsuit was brought by the Bay Island Action Committee against the Board of Estimate in which the plaintiff sought withdrawal of approval of housing for the elderly in the Bay Island area given by the Board in 2005.

    A. 8-3:1   B. 8-5:1   C. 8-3:B1   D. 8-5:E1

4. In December 2004, community leaders asked the Police Department to ban outdoor meetings of a religious group on the grounds that the meetings were disrupting the area. Such meetings had been held from time to time during 2004. On January 31, 2005, the Police Department asked the government legal office for an opinion on whether granting this request would violate the worshippers' right to freedom of religion.

    A. 2-4:G-1   B. 2-5:G1   C. 2-5:B-1   D. 2-4:B1

5. In 2004, a woman filed suit against the Board of Elections. She alleged that she had not been permitted to vote at her usual polling place in the 2003 election and had been told she was not registered there. She claimed that she had always voted there and that her record card had been lost. This was the fourth case of its type for this agency.

    A. 6-4:4   B. 6-3:C4   C. 3-4:6   D. 6-3:4

6. A lawsuit was brought in 2001 by the Ace Pinball Machine Company against the Commissioner of Consumer Affairs. The lawsuit contested an ordinance which banned the use of pinball machines on the ground that they are gambling devices.
    This was the third lawsuit to which the Department of Consumer Affairs was a party.

    A. 4-1:1   B. 4-3:F1   C. 4-1:3   D. 3F-4:1

7. You are instructed by your supervisor to type a statement that must be signed by the per- 7._____
son making the statement and by three witnesses to the signature. The typed statement
will take two pages and will leave no room for signatures if the normal margin is maintained at the bottom of the second page.
In this situation, the PREFERRED method is to type

    A. the signature lines below the normal margin on the second page
    B. nothing further and have the witnesses sign without a typed signature line
    C. the signature lines on a third page
    D. some of the text and the signature lines on a third page

8. Certain legal documents always begin with a statement of venue - that is, the county and 8._____
state in which the document is executed. This is usually boxed with a parentheses or
colons.
The one of the following documents that ALWAYS bears a statement of venue in a
prominent position at its head is a(n)

    A. affidavit   B. memorandum of law
    C. contract of sale   D. will

9. You are requested to take stenographic notes and to transcribe the statements of a per- 9._____
son under oath. The person has a heavy accent and speaks in ungrammatical and bro-
ken English.
When you are transcribing the testimony, of the following, the BEST thing for you to do
is to

    A. transcribe the testimony exactly as spoken, making no grammatical changes
    B. make only the grammatical changes which would clarify the client's statements
    C. make all grammatical changes so that the testimony is in standard English form
    D. ask the client's permission before making any grammatical changes

10. When the material typed on a printed form does not fill the space provided, a Z-ruling is 10._____
frequently drawn to fill up the unused space.
The MAIN purpose of this practice is to

    A. make the document more pleasing to the eye
    B. indicate that the preceding material is correct
    C. insure that the document is not altered
    D. show that the lawyer has read it

11. After you had typed an original and five copies of a certain document, some changes 11._____
were made in ink on the original and were initialed by all the parties. The original was
signed by all the parties, and the signatures were notarized.
Which of the following should *generally* be typed on the copies BEFORE filing the original and the copies? The inked changes

    A. but not the signatures, initials, or notarial data
    B. the signatures and the initials but not the notarial data
    C. and the notarial data but not the signatures or initials
    D. the signatures, the initials, and the notarial data

12. The first paragraph of a noncourt agreement *generally* contains all of the following EXCEPT the   12

    A. specific terms of the agreement
    B. date of the agreement
    C. purpose of the agreement
    D. names of the parties involved

13. When typing an answer in a court proceeding, the place where the word ANSWER should be typed on the first page of the document is   13

    A. at the upper left-hand corner
    B. below the index number and to the right of the box containing the names of the parties to the action
    C. above the index number and to the right of the box containing the names of the parties to the action
    D. to the left of the names of the attorneys for the defendant

14. Which one of the following statements BEST describes the legal document called an acknowledgment?   14
It is

    A. an answer to an affidavit
    B. a receipt issued by the court when a document is filed
    C. proof of service of a summons
    D. a declaration that a signature is valid

15. Suppose you typed the original and three carbon copies of a legal document which was dictated by an attorney in your office. He has already signed the original copy, and corrections have been made on all copies.   15
Regarding the carbon copies, which one of the following procedures is the PROPER one to follow?

    A. Leave the signature line blank on the carbon copies
    B. Ask the attorney to sign the carbon copies
    C. Print or type the attorney's name on the signature line on the carbon copies
    D. Sign your name to the carbon copies followed by the attorney's initials

16. Suppose your office is defending a particular person in a court action. This person comes to the office and asks to see some of the lawyer's working papers in his file. The lawyer assigned to the case is out of the office at the time.   16
You SHOULD

    A. permit him to examine his entire file as long as he does not remove any materials from it
    B. make an appointment for the caller to come back later when the lawyer will be there
    C. ask him what working papers he wants to see and show him only those papers
    D. tell him that he needs written permission from the lawyer in order to see any records

17. Suppose that you receive a phone call from an official who is annoyed about a letter from   17.____
your office which she just received. The lawyer who dictated the letter is not in the office
at the moment.
Of the following, the BEST action for you to take is to

    A. explain that the lawyer is out but that you will ask the lawyer to return her call when
he returns
    B. take down all of the details of her complaint and tell her that you will get back to her
with an explanation
    C. refer to the proper file so that you can give her an explanation of the reasons for the
letter over the phone
    D. make an appointment for her to stop by the office to speak with the lawyer

18. Suppose that you have taken dictation for an interoffice memorandum. You are asked to   18.____
prepare it for distribution to four lawyers in your department whose names are given to
you. You will type an original and four carbon copies. Which one of the following is COR-
RECT with regard to the typing of the lawyers' names?
The names of all of the lawyers should appear

    A. *only* on the original
    B. on the original and each copy should have the name of one lawyer
    C. on each of the copies but not on the original
    D. on the original and on all of the copies

19. Regarding the correct typing of punctuation, the GENERALLY accepted practice is that   19.____
there should be

    A. two spaces after a semi-colon
    B. one space before an apostrophe used in the body of a word
    C. no space between parentheses and the matter enclosed
    D. one space before and after a hyphen

20. Suppose you have just completed typing an original and two copies of a letter   20.____
requesting information. The original is to be signed by a lawyer in your office. The first
copy is for the files, and the second is to be used as a reminder to follow up.
The PROPER time to file the file copy of the letter is

    A. after the letter has been signed and corrections have been made on the copies
    B. before you take the letter to the lawyer for his signature
    C. after a follow-up letter has been sent
    D. after a response to the letter has been received

21. A secretary in a legal office has just typed a letter. She has typed the copy distribution   21.____
notation on the copies to indicate *blind copy distribution*. This *blind copy* notation shows
that

    A. copies of the letter are being sent to persons that the addressee does not know
    B. copies of the letter are being sent to other persons without the addressee's knowledge
    C. a copy of the letter will be enlarged for a legally blind person
    D. a copy of the letter is being given as an extra copy to the addressee

22. Suppose that one of the attorneys in your office dictates material to you without indicating punctuation. He has asked that you give him, as soon as possible, a single copy of a rough draft to be triple-spaced so that he can make corrections.
Of the following, what is the BEST thing for you to do in this situation?

    A. Assume that no punctuation is desired in the material
    B. Insert the punctuation as you type the rough draft
    C. Transcribe the material exactly as dictated, but attach a note to the attorney stating your suggested changes
    D. Before you start to type the draft, tell the attorney you want to read back your notes so that he can indicate punctuation

23. When it is necessary to type a mailing notation such as CERTIFIED, REGISTERED, or FEDEX on an envelope, the GENERALLY accepted place to type it is

    A. directly above the address
    B. in the area below where the stamp will be affixed
    C. in the lower left-hand corner
    D. in the upper left-hand corner

24. When taking a citation of a case in shorthand, which of the following should you write FIRST if you are having difficulty keeping up with the dictation?

    A. Volume and page number   B. Title of volume
    C. Name of plaintiff   D. Name of defendant

25. All of the following abbreviations and their meanings are correctly paired EXCEPT

    A. viz. - namely   B. ibid. - refer
    C. n.b. - note well   D. q.v. - which see

KEY (CORRECT ANSWERS)

1.	D	11.	D
2.	D	12.	A
3.	B	13.	B
4.	B	14.	D
5.	A	15.	C
6.	C	16.	B
7.	D	17.	A
8.	A	18.	D
9.	A	19.	C
10.	C	20.	A

21.	B
22.	B
23.	B
24.	A
25.	B

EXAMINATION SECTION
TEST 1

DIRECTIONS: Each question or incomplete statement is followed by
several suggested answers or completions. Select the
one that BEST answers the question or completes the
statement. *PRINT THE LETTER OF THE CORRECT ANSWER IN
THE SPACE AT THE RIGHT.*

1. Records of one type or another are kept in every office.   1.___
    The MOST important of the following reasons for the
    supervisor of a clerical or stenographic unit to keep
    statistical records of the work done in his unit is
    generally to
    A. supply basic information needed in planning the work
       of the unit
    B. obtain statistics for comparison with other units .
    C. serve as the basis for unsatisfactory employee
       evaluation
    D. provide the basis for special research projects on
       program budgeting

2. It is better for an employee to report and be responsible   2.___
    directly to several supervisors than to report and be
    responsible to only one supervisor.
    This statement directly CONTRADICTS the supervisory prin-
    ciple generally known as
    A. span of control   B. unity of command
    C. delegation of authority D. accountability

3. The one of the following which would MOST likely lead to   3.___
    friction among clerks in a unit is for the unit super-
    visor to
    A. defend the actions of his clerks when discussing them
       with his own supervisor
    B. praise each of his clerks *in confidence* as the best
       clerk in the unit
    C. get his men to work together as a team in completing
       the work of the unit
    D. consider the point of view of the rank and file
       clerks when assigning unpleasant tasks

4. You become aware that one of the employees you supervise   4.___
    has failed to follow correct procedure and has been
    permitting various reports to be prepared, typed, and
    transmitted improperly.
    The BEST action for you to take FIRST in this situation
    is to
    A. order the employee to review all departmental pro-
       cedures and reprimand him for having violated them
    B. warn the employee that he must obey regulations
       because uniformity is essential for effective
       departmental operation

    C. confer with the employee both about his failure to
       follow regulations and his reasons for doing so
    D. watch the employee's work very closely in the future
       but say nothing about this violation

5. The supervisory clerk who would be MOST likely to have   5.__
   poor control over his subordinates is the one who
    A. goes to unusually great lengths to try to win their
       approval
    B. pitches in with the work they are doing during
       periods of heavy workload when no extra help can be
       obtained
    C. encourages and helps his subordinates toward advance-
       ment
    D. considers suggestions from his subordinates before
       establishing new work procedures involving them

6. Suppose that a clerk who has been transferred to your   6.__
   office from another division in your agency because of
   difficulties with his supervisor has been placed under
   your supervision.
   The BEST course of action for you to take FIRST is to
    A. instruct the clerk in the duties he will be per-
       forming in your office and make him feel *wanted* in
       his new position
    B. analyze the clerk's past grievance to determine if
       the transfer was the best solution to the problem
    C. advise him of the difficulties his former super-
       visor had with other employees and encourage him
       not to feel bad about the transfer
    D. warn him that you will not tolerate any nonsense
       and that he will be under continuous surveillance
       while assigned to you

7. A certain office supervisor takes the initiative to   7.__
   represent his employees' interests related to working
   conditions, opportunities for advancement, etc. to his
   own supervisor and the administrative levels of the
   agency.
   This supervisor's actions will MOST probably have the
   effect of
    A. preventing employees from developing individual
       initiative in their work goals
    B. encouraging employees to compete openly for the
       special attention of their supervisor
    C. depriving employees of the opportunity to be
       represented by persons and/or unions of their own
       choosing
    D. building employee confidence in their supervisor
       and a spirit of cooperation in their work

8. Suppose that you have been promoted, assigned as a super-   8.___
   visor of a certain unit, and asked to reorganize its
   functions so that specific routine procedures can be
   established.
   Before deciding which routines to establish, the FIRST
   of the following steps you should take is to
      A. decide who will perform each task in the routine
      B. determine the purpose to be served by each routine
         procedure
      C. outline the sequence of steps in each routine to be
         established
      D. calculate if more staff will be needed to carry out
         the new procedures

9. When routine procedures covering the ordinary work of an   9.___
   office are established, the supervisor of the office tends
   to be relieved of the need to
      A. make repeated decisions on the handling of recurring
         similar situations
      B. check the accuracy of the work completed by his
         subordinates
      C. train his subordinates in new work procedures
      D. plan and schedule the work of his office

10. Of the following, the method which would be LEAST help-   10.___
    ful to a supervisor in effectively applying the princi-
    ples of on-the-job safety to the daily work of his unit
    is for him to
       A. initiate corrections of unsafe layouts of equipment
          and unsafe work processes
       B. take charge of operations that are not routine to
          make certain that safety precautions are established
          and observed
       C. continue to *talk safety* and promote safety conscious-
          ness in his subordinates
       D. figure the cost of all accidents which could possi-
          bly occur on the job

11. A clerk is assigned to serve as receptionist for a large   11.___
    and busy office. Although many members of the public
    visit this office, the clerk often experiences periods
    of time in which he has nothing to do.
    In these circumstances, the MOST advisable of the
    following actions for the supervisor to take is to
       A. assign a number of relatively low priority clerical
          jobs to the receptionist to do in the slow periods
       B. regularly rotate this assignment so that all of the
          clerks experience this lighter work load
       C. assign the receptionist job as part of the duties
          of a number of clerks whose desks are nearest the
          reception room
       D. overlook the situation since most of the recep-
          tionist's time is spent in performing a necessary
          and meaningful function

12. For a supervisor to require all stenographers in a stenographic pool to produce the same amount of work on a particular day is

    A. *advisable* since it will prove that the supervisor plays no favorites

    B. *fair* since all the stenographers are receiving approximately the same salary, their output should be equivalent

    C. *not necessary* since the fast workers will compensate for the slow workers

    D. *not realistic* since individual differences in abilities and work assignment must be taken into consideration

12._

13. The establishment of a centralized typing pool to service the various units in an organization is MOST likely to be worthwhile when there is

    A. wide fluctuation from time to time in the needs of the various units for typing service

    B. a large volume of typing work to be done in each of the units

    C. a need by each unit for different kinds of typing service

    D. a training program in operation to develop and maintain typing skills

13._

14. A newly appointed supervisor should learn as much as possible about the backgrounds of his subordinates. This statement is GENERALLY correct because

    A. knowing their backgrounds assures they will be treated objectively, equally, and without favor

    B. effective handling of subordinates is based upon knowledge of their individual differences

    C. subordinates perform more efficiently under one supervisor than under another

    D. subordinates have confidence in a supervisor who knows all about them

14._

15. The use of electronic computers in modern businesses has produced many changes in office and information management.
Of the following, it would NOT be correct to state that computer utilization

    A. broadens the scope of managerial and supervisory authority

    B. establishes uniformity in the processing and reporting of information

    C. cuts costs by reducing the personnel needed for efficient office operation

    D. supplies management rapidly with up-to-date data to facilitate decision-making

15._

16. The CHIEF advantage of having a single, large open   16.___
    office instead of small partitioned ones for a clerical
    unit or stenographic pool is that the single, large
    open office
    A. affords privacy without isolation for all office
       workers not directly dealing with the public
    B. assures the smoother, more continuous inter-office
       flow of work that is essential for efficient work
       production
    C. facilitates the office supervisor's visual control
       over and communication with his subordinates
    D. permits a more decorative and functional arrangement
       of office furniture and machines

17. When a supervisor provides a new employee with the infor-   17.___
    mation necessary for a basic knowledge and a general
    understanding of practices and procedures of the agency,
    he is applying the type of training generally known as
    _____ training.
    A. pre-employment   B. induction
    C. on-the-job   D. supervisory

18. Many government agencies require the approval by a   18.___
    central forms control unit of the design and reproduction
    of new office forms.
    The one of the following results of this procedure that
    is a DISADVANTAGE is that requiring prior approval of a
    central forms control unit usually
    A. limits the distribution of forms to those offices
       with justifiable reasons for receiving them
    B. permits checking whether existing forms or modifi-
       cations of them are in line with current agency
       needs
    C. encourages reliance on only the central office to
       set up all additional forms when needed
    D. provides for someone with a specialized knowledge
       of forms design to review and criticize new and
       revised forms

19. Suppose that a large quantity of information is in the   19.___
    files which are located a good distance from your desk.
    Almost every worker in your office must use these files
    constantly. Your duties in particular require that you
    daily refer to about 25 of the same items. They are
    short, one-page items distributed throughout the files.
    In this situation, your BEST course would be to
    A. take the items that you use daily from the files
       and keep them on your desk, inserting *out cards*
       in their place
    B. go to the files each time you need the information
       so that the items will be there when other workers
       need them
    C. make xerox copies of the information you use most
       frequently and keep them in your desk for ready
       reference

D. label the items you use most often with different colored tabs for immediate identification

20. Of the following, the MOST important advantage of preparing manuals of office procedures in loose-leaf form is that this form
    A. permits several employees to use different sections simultaneously
    B. facilitates the addition of new material and the removal of obsolete material
    C. is more readily arranged in alphabetical order
    D. reduces the need for cross-references to locate material carried under several headings

20.___

21. Suppose that you establish a new clerical procedure for the unit you supervise. Your keeping a close check on the time required by your staff to handle the new procedure is WISE mainly because such a check will find out
    A. whether your subordinates know how to handle the new procedure
    B. whether a revision of the unit's work schedule will be necessary as a result of the new procedure
    C. what attitude your employees have toward the new procedure
    D. what alterations in job descriptions will be necessitated by the new procedure

21.___

22. From the viewpoint of an office supervisor, the BEST of the following reasons for distributing the incoming mail before the beginning of the regular work day is that
    A. distribution can be handled quickly and most efficiently at that time
    B. distribution later in the day may be distracting to or interfere with other employees
    C. the employees who distribute the mail can then perform other tasks during the rest of the day
    D. office activities for the day based on the mail may then be started promptly

22.___

23. Suppose you are the head of a unit with 10 staff members who are located in several different rooms.
    If you want to inform your staff of a minor change in procedure, the BEST and LEAST expensive way of doing so would usually be to
    A. send a mimeographed copy to each staff member
    B. call a special staff meeting and announce the change
    C. circulate a memo, having each staff member initial it
    D. have a clerk tell each member of the staff about the change

23.___

24. The numbered statements below relate to the stenographic   24.___
    skill of taking dictation. According to authorities on
    secretarial practices, which of these are generally
    recommended guides to development of efficient steno-
    graphic skills?
       I. A stenographer should date her notebook daily to
          facilitate locating certain notes at a later time.
      II. A stenographer should make corrections of gramma-
          tical mistakes while her boss is dictating to her.
     III. A stenographer should draw a line through the
          dictated matter in her notebook after she has
          transcribed it.
      IV. A stenographer should write in longhand unfamiliar
          names and addresses dictated to her.

    The CORRECT answer is:
       A. Only Statements I, II, and III are generally
          recommended guides.
       B. Only Statements II, III, and IV are generally
          recommended guides.
       C. Only Statements I, III, and IV are generally
          recommended guides.
       D. All four statements are generally recommended guides.

25. A bureau of a city agency is about to move to a new   25.___
    location.
    Of the following, the FIRST step that should be taken
    in order to provide a good layout for the office at the
    new location is to
       A. decide the exact amount of space to be assigned to
          each unit of the bureau
       B. decide whether to lay out a single large open office
          or one consisting of small partitioned units
       C. ask each unit chief in the bureau to examine the
          new location and submit a request for the amount of
          space he needs
       D. prepare a detailed plan of the dimensions of the
          floor space to be occupied by the bureau at the new
          location

26. Of the following, the BEST reason for discarding a sheet   26.___
    of carbon paper is that
       A. some carbon rubs off on your fingers when handled
       B. there are several creases in the sheet
       C. the short edge of the sheet is curled
       D. the finish on the sheet is smooth and shiny

27. Suppose you are the supervisor of the mailroom of a   27.___
    large city agency where the mail received daily is opened
    by machine, sorted by hand for delivery, and time-stamped.
    Letters and any enclosures are removed from envelopes and
    stapled together before distribution. One of your newest
    clerks asks you what should be done when a letter makes
    reference to an enclosure, but no enclosure is in the
    envelope.

You should tell him that, in this situation, the BEST
procedure is to
   A. make an entry of the sender's name and address in the
      missing enclosures file and forward the letter to its
      proper destination
   B. return the letter to its sender, attaching a request
      for the missing enclosure
   C. put the letter aside until a proper investigation
      may be made concerning the missing enclosure
   D. route the letter to the person for whom it is
      intended, noting the absence of the enclosure on the
      letter-margin

28. The term *work flow*, when used in connection with office   28.__
    management or the activities in an office, GENERALLY
    means the
       A. use of charts in the analysis of various office
          functions
       B. rate of speed at which work flows through a single
          section of an office
       C. step-by-step physical routing of work through its
          various procedures
       D. number of individual work units which can be pro-
          duced by the average employee

29. Physical conditions can have a definite effect on the   29.__
    efficiency and morale of an office.
    Which of the following statements about physical condi-
    tions in an office is CORRECT?
       A. Hard, non-porous surfaces reflect more noise than
          linoleum on the top of a desk.
       B. Painting in tints of bright yellow is more appro-
          priate for sunny, well-lit offices than for dark,
          poorly-lit offices.
       C. Plate glass is better than linoleum for the top of
          a desk.
       D. The central typing room needs less light than a
          conference room does.

30. In a certain filing system, documents are consecutively   30.__
    numbered as they are filed, a register is maintained of
    such consecutively numbered documents, and a record is
    kept of the number of each document removed from the
    files and its destination.
    This system will NOT help in
       A. finding the present whereabouts of a particular
          document
       B. proving the accuracy of the data recorded on a
          certain document
       C. indicating whether observed existing documents were
          ever filed
       D. locating a desired document without knowing what its
          contents are

31. In deciding the kind and number of records an agency   31.___
    should keep, the administrative staff must recognize
    that records are of value in office management PRIMARILY
    as
       A. informational bases for agency activities
       B. data for evaluating the effectiveness of the agency
       C. raw material on which statistical analyses are to
          be based
       D. evidence that the agency is carrying out its duties
          and responsibilities

32. Complaints are often made by the public about the   32.___
    government's procedures. Although in most cases such
    procedures cannot be changed since various laws and
    regulations require them, it may still be possible to
    reduce the number of complaints.
    Which one of the following actions by personnel dealing
    with applicants for city services is LEAST likely to
    reduce complaints concerning city procedures?
       A. Treating all citizens alike and explaining to them
          that no exceptions to required procedures can be
          made
       B. Explaining briefly to the citizen why he should
          comply with regulations
       C. Being careful to avoid mistakes which may make
          additional interviews or correspondence necessary
       D. Keeping the citizen informed of the progress of his
          correspondence when immediate disposition cannot be
          made

33. Persons whose native language is not English sometimes   33.___
    experience difficulty in communication when visiting
    public offices.
    The MOST common method used by such persons to overcome
    the difficulty in communication is to
       A. write in their own language whatever they wish to say
       B. hire a professional interpreter
       C. ask a patrolman for assistance
       D. bring with them an English-speaking friend or relative

34. In answering a complaint made by a member of the public   34.___
    that a certain essential procedure required by your
    agency is difficult to follow, it would be BEST for you
    to stress most
       A. that a change in the rules may be considered if
          enough complaints are received
       B. why the operation of a large agency sometimes proves
          a hardship in individual cases
       C. the necessity for the procedure
       D. the origin of the procedure

35. When talking to a citizen, it is BEST for an employee of   35.___
    government to
    A. use ordinary conversational phrases and a natural
       manner
    B. try to copy the pronunciation and level of education
       shown by the citizen
    C. try to speak in a very cultured manner and tone
    D. use technical terms to show his familiarity with
       his own work

36. Employees who service the public should maintain an   36.___
    attitude which is both sympathetic and objective.
    An unsympathetic and subjective attitude would be shown
    by a public employee who
    A. says *no* with a smile when a citizen's request must
       be denied
    B. listens attentively to a long complaint from a
       citizen about government's *red tape*
    C. responds with sarcasm when a citizen asks a question
       which has an obvious manner
    D. suggests a definite solution to a citizen's problems

37. Of the following methods of conducting an interview,   37.___
    the BEST is to
    A. ask questions with *yes* or *no* answers
    B. listen carefully and ask only questions that are
       pertinent
    C. fire questions at the interviewee so that he must
       answer sincerely and briefly
    D. read standardized questions to the person being
       interviewed

38. An interviewer should begin with topics which are easy   38.___
    to talk about and which are not threatening.
    This procedure is useful MAINLY because it
    A. allows the applicant a little time to get accustomed
       to the situation and leads to freer communication
    B. distracts the attention of the person being inter-
       viewed from the main purpose of the questioning
    C. is the best way for the interviewer to show that he
       is relaxed and confident on the job
    D. causes the interviewee to feel that the interviewer
       is apportioning valuable questioning time

39. The initial interview will normally be more of a problem   39.___
    to the interviewer than any subsequent interviews he may
    have with the same person because
    A. the interviewee is likely to be hostile
    B. there is too much to be accomplished in one session
    C. he has less information about the client than he
       will have later
    D. some information may be forgotten when later making
       record of this first interview

40. You are a supervisor in an agency and are holding your   40.___
    first interview with a new employee.
    In this interview, you should strive MAINLY to
    A. show the new employee that you are an efficient and
       objective supervisor, with a completely impersonal
       attitude toward your subordinate
    B. complete the entire orientation process including
       the giving of detailed job-duty instructions
    C. make it clear to the employee that all your deci-
       sions are based on your many years of experience
    D. lay the groundwork for a good employee-supervisor
       relationship by gaining the new employee's confidence

41. Most successful interviews are those in which the inter-   41.___
    viewer shows a genuine interest in the person he is
    questioning.
    This attitude would MOST likely cause the individual
    being interviewed to
    A. feel that the interviewer already knows all the facts
       in his case
    B. act more naturally and reveal more of his true
       feelings
    C. request that the interviewer give more attention to
       his problems, not his personality
    D. react defensively, suppress his negative feelings,
       and conceal the real facts in his case

42. Questions worded so that the person being interviewed   42.___
    has some hint of the desired answer can modify the
    person's response.
    The result of the inclusion of such questions in an
    interview, even when they are used inadvertently, is to
    A. have no effect on the basic content of the informa-
       tion given by the person interviewed
    B. have value in convincing the person that the
       suggested plan is the best for him
    C. cause the person to give more meaningful informa-
       tion
    D. reduce the validity of the information obtained
       from the person

43. The person MOST likely to be a good interviewer is one   43.___
    who
    A. is able to outguess the person being interviewed
    B. tries to change the attitudes of the persons he
       interviews
    C. controls the interview by skillfully dominating
       the conversation
    D. is able to imagine himself in the position of the
       person being interviewed

44. The *halo effect* is an overall impression on the inter-   44.__
viewer, whether favorable or unfavorable, usually created
by a single trait. This impression then influences the
appraisal of all other factors.
A *halo effect* is LEAST likely to be created at an inter-
view where the interviewee is a
   A. person of average appearance and ability
   B. rough-looking man who uses abusive language
   C. young attractive woman being interviewed by a man
   D. person who demonstrates an exceptional ability to
      remember facts

45. Of the following, the BEST way for an interviewer to   45.__
calm a person who seems to have become emotionally upset
as a result of a question asked is for the interviewer to
   A. talk to the person about other things for a short
      time
   B. ask that the person control himself
   C. probe for the cause of his emotional upset
   D. finish the questioning as quickly as possible

46. Of the following, a centralized filing system is LEAST   46.__
suitable for filing
   A. material which is confidential in nature
   B. routine correspondence
   C. periodic reports of the divisions of the department
   D. material used by several divisions of the department

47. Form letters should be used MAINLY when   47.__
   A. an office has to reply to a great many similar
      inquiries
   B. the type of correspondence varies widely
   C. it is necessary to have letters which are well-
      phrased and grammatically correct
   D. letters of inquiry have to be answered as soon as
      possible after they are received

48. Suppose that you are assigned to prepare a form from   48.__
which certain information will be posted in a ledger.
It would be MOST helpful to the person posting the
information in the ledger if, in designing the form,
you were to
   A. use the same color paper for both the form and the
      ledger
   B. make the form the same size as the pages of the
      ledger
   C. have the information on the form in the same order
      as that used in the ledger
   D. include in the form a box which is to be initialed
      when the data on the form have been posted in the
      ledger

49. A misplaced record is a lost record.
Of the following, the MOST valid implication of this statement in regard to office work is that
    A. all records in an office should be filed in strict alphabetical order
    B. accuracy in filing is essential
    C. only one method of filing should be used throughout the office
    D. files should be locked when not in use

49.___

50. James Jones is applying for a provisional appointment as a clerk in your department. He presents a letter of recommendation from a former employer stating: *James Jones was rarely late or absent; he has a very pleasing manner and never got into an argument with his fellow employees.*
The above information concerning this applicant
    A. proves clearly that he produces more work than the average employee
    B. indicates that he was probably attempting to conceal his inefficiency from his former employer
    C. presents no conclusive evidence of his ability to do clerical work
    D. indicates clearly that with additional training he will make a good supervisor

50.___

KEY (CORRECT ANSWERS)

1. A	11. A	21. B	31. A	41. B
2. B	12. D	22. D	32. A	42. D
3. B	13. A	23. C	33. D	43. D
4. C	14. B	24. C	34. C	44. A
5. A	15. A	25. D	35. A	45. A
6. A	16. C	26. B	36. C	46. A
7. D	17. B	27. D	37. B	47. A
8. B	18. C	28. C	38. A	48. C
9. A	19. C	29. A	39. C	49. B
10. D	20. B	30. B	40. D	50. C

TEST 2

Questions 1-10.

1. Whether one depends on flourescent or artificial light or   1.__
   both, adequate standards should be maintained by means
   of systematic tests.
   - A. natural   B. safeguards
   - C. established   D. routine

2. A policeman has to be prepared to assume his knowledge   2.__
   as a social scientist in the community.
   - A. forced   B. role
   - C. philosopher   D. street

3. It is practically impossible to tell whether a sentence   3.__
   is very long simply by measuring its length.
   - A. almost   B. mark   C. too   D. denoting

4. By using carbon paper, the typist easily is able to   4.__
   insert as many as six copies of a report.
   - A. adding   B. seldom   C. make   D. forms

5. Although all people have many traits in common, a recep-   5.__
   tionist in her agreements with people learns quickly how
   different each person is from every other person.
   - A. impressions   B. associations
   - C. decides   D. various

6. Strong leaders are required to organize a community for   6.__
   delinquency prevention and for dissemination of organized
   crime and drug addiction.
   - A. tactics   B. important   C. control   D. meetings

7. The demonstrators, who were taken to the Criminal Courts   7.___
    building in Manhattan (because it was large enough to
    accommodate them), contended that the arrests were
    unwarrented.
        A. demonstraters   B. Manhatten
        C. accomodate   D. unwarranted

8. When two or more forms for spelling a word exist, it is   8.___
    advisable to use the preferred spelling indicated in the
    dictionary, and to use it consistantly.
        A. adviseable   B. prefered
        C. dictionery   D. consistently

9. If you know the language of the foreign country you are   9.___
    visiting, your embarassment will disappear and you will
    learn a lot more about the customs and characteristics
    of the common people.
        A. foriegn   B. embarrassment
        C. dissappear   D. charactaristics

10. Material consisting of government bulletins, advertice-   10.___
    ments, catalogues, announcements of address changes and
    any other periodical material of this nature, may be
    filed alphabetically according to subject.
        A. advertisements   B. cataloges
        C. periodicle   D. alphabeticly

Questions 11-14.

DIRECTIONS: Each of the two sentences in Questions 11 through 14
               may contain errors in punctuation, capitalization, or
               grammar.

               If there is an error in only Sentence I, mark your
               answer A.
               If there is an error in only Sentence II, mark your
               answer B.
               If there is an error in both Sentences I and II, mark
               your answer C.
               If both Sentences I and II are correct, mark your
               answer D.

11.   I. It is very annoying to have a pencil sharpener,   11.___
          which is not in proper working order.
      II. The building watchman checked the door of Charlie's
          office and found that the lock has been jammed.

12.   I. Since he went on the New York City council a year   12.___
          ago, one of his primary concerns has been safety
          in the streets.
      II. After waiting in the doorway for about 15 minutes,
          a black sedan appeared.

13.   I. When you are studying a good textbook is important.   13.___
    II. He said he would divide the money equally between you and me.

14.   I. The question is, "How can a large number of envelopes   14.___
     be sealed rapidly without the use of a sealing machine?"
    II. The administrator assigned two stenographers, Mary and I, to the new bureau.

Questions 15-16.

DIRECTIONS: In each of Questions 15 and 16, the four sentences are from a paragraph in a report. They are not in the right order. Which of the following arrangements is the BEST one?

15. 1. An executive may answer a letter by writing his reply   15.__
    on the face of the letter itself instead of having a return letter typed.
   2. This procedure is efficient because it saves the executive's time, the typist's time, and saves office file space.
   3. Copying machines are used in small offices as well as large offices to save time and money in making brief replies to business letters.
   4. A copy is made on a copying machine to go into the company files, while the original is mailed back to the sender.

    The CORRECT answer is:
     A. 1, 2, 4, 3   B. 1, 4, 2, 3
     C. 3, 1, 4, 2   D. 3, 4, 2, 1

16. 1. Most organizations favor one of the types but always   16._
    include the others to a lesser degree.
   2. However, we can detect a definite trend toward greater use of symbolic control.
   3. We suggest that our local police agencies are today primarily utilizing material control.
   4. Control can be classified into three types: physical, material, and symbolic.

    The CORRECT answer is:
     A. 4, 2, 3, 1   B. 2, 1, 4, 3
     C. 3, 4, 2, 1   D. 4, 1, 3, 2

17.   Of the following, the MOST effective report writing   17._
    style is usually characterized by
     A. covering all the main ideas in the same paragraph
     B. presenting each significant point in a new paragraph
     C. placing the least important points before the most important points
     D. giving all points equal emphasis throughout the report

18. Of the following, which factor is COMMON to all types of   18.___
    reports?
    A. Presentation of information
    B. Interpretation of findings
    C. Chronological ordering of the information
    D. Presentation of conclusions and recommendations

19. When writing a report, the one of the following which   19.___
    you should do FIRST is
    A. set up a logical work schedule
    B. determine your objectives in writing the report
    C. select your statistical material
    D. obtain the necessary data from the files

20. Generally, the frequency with which reports are to be   20.___
    submitted or the length of the interval which they cover
    should depend MAINLY on the
    A. amount of time needed to prepare the reports
    B. degree of comprehensiveness required in the reports
    C. availability of the data to be included in the
       reports
    D. extent of the variations in the data with the passage
       of time

21. The objectiveness of a report is its unbiased presenta-   21.___
    tion of the facts.
    If this be so, which of the following reports listed
    below is likely to be the MOST objective?
    A. The Best Use of an Electronic Computer in Department Z
    B. The Case for Raising the Salaries of Employees in
       Department A
    C. Quarterly Summary of Production in the Duplicating
       Unit of Department Y
    D. Recommendation to Terminate Employee X's Services
       Because of Misconduct

Questions 22-27.

DIRECTIONS: Questions 22 through 27 are to be answered SOLELY on the basis of the information contained in the charts below which relate to the budget allocations of City X, a small suburban community. The charts depict the annual budget allocations by Department and by Expenditures over a five-year period.

CITY X BUDGET IN MILLIONS OF DOLLARS

TABLE I. Budget Allocations By Department

Department	1997	1998	1999	2000	2001
Public Safety	30	45	50	40	50
Health and Welfare	50	75	90	60	70
Engineering	5	8	10	5	8
Human Resources	10	12	20	10	22
Conversation and Environment	10	15	20	20	15
Education and Development	15	25	35	15	15
TOTAL BUDGET	120	180	225	150	180

TABLE II. Budget Allocations By Expenditures

Category	1997	1998	1999	2000	2001
Raw Materials and Machinery	36	63	68	30	98
Capital Outlay	12	27	56	15	18
Personal Services	72	90	101	105	64
TOTAL BUDGET	120	180	225	150	180

22. The year in which the SMALLEST percentage of the total annual budget was allocated to the Department of Education and Development is
A. 1997　B. 1998　C. 2000　D. 2001

23. Assume that, in 2000, the Department of Conservation and Environment divided its annual budget into the three categories of expenditures and in exactly the same proportion as the budget shown in Table II for the year 2000.
The amount allocated for capital outlay in the Department of Conservation and Environment's 2000 budget was MOST NEARLY _____ million.
A. $2　B. $4　C. $6　D. $10

24. From the year 1998 to the year 2000, the sum of the   24.___
    annual budgets for the Departments of Public Safety and
    Engineering showed an overall _____ of _____ million.
        A. decline; $8   B. increase; $7
        C. decline; $15   D. increase; $22

25. The LARGEST dollar increase in departmental budget   25.___
    allocations from one year to the next was in
        A. Public Safety from 1997 to 1998
        B. Health and Welfare from 1997 to 1998
        C. Education and Development from 1999 to 2000
        D. Human Resources from 1999 to 2000

26. During the five-year period, the annual budget of the   26.___
    Department of Human Resources was GREATER than the
    annual budget for the Department of Conservation and
    Environment in _____ of the years.
        A. none   B. one   C. two   D. three

27. If the total City X budget increases at the same rate   27.___
    from 2001 to 2002 as it did from 2000 to 2001, the total
    City X budget for 2002 will be MOST NEARLY _____ million.
        A. $180   B. $200   C. $210   D. $215

Questions 28-34.

DIRECTIONS: Questions 28 through 34 are to be answered SOLELY on
             the basis of the information contained in the graph
             below which relates to the work of a public agency.

No. of
work units
completed

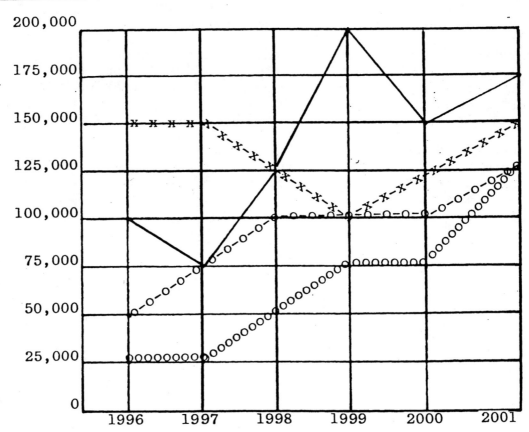

Units of each type of work completed by a public agency from
1996 to 2001.

Letters Written ─────────

Documents Filed ─x─x─x─x─x─x

Applications Processed ─o─o─o─o─o─o

Inspections made ooooooooooooo

28. The year for which the number of units of one type of   28.___
    work completed was LESS than it was for the previous
    year while the number of each of the other types of
    work completed was MORE than it was for the previous
    year was
    A. 1997   B. 1998   C. 1999   D. 2000

29. The number of letters written EXCEEDED the number of   29.___
    applications processed by the same amount in _____ of
    the years.
    A. two   B. three   C. four   D. five

30. The year in which the number of each type of work com-   30.___
    pleted was GREATER than in the preceding year was
    A. 1998   B. 1999   C. 2000   D. 2001

31. The number of applications processed and the number of   31.___
    documents filed were the SAME in
    A. 1997   B. 1998   C. 1999   D. 2000

32. The TOTAL number of units of work completed by the   32.___
    agency
    A. increased in each year after 1996
    B. decreased from the prior year in two of the years
       after 1996
    C. was the same in two successive years from 1996 to
       2001
    D. was less in 1996 than in any of the following years

33. For the year in which the number of letters written was   33.___
    twice as high as it was in 1996, the number of documents
    filed was _____ it was in 1996.
    A. the same as   B. two-thirds of what
    C. five-sixths of what   D. 1½ times what

34. The variable which was the MOST stable during the   34.___
    period 1996 through 2001 was
    A. Inspections Made   B. Letters Written
    C. Documents Filed   D. Applications Processed

Questions 35-41.

DIRECTIONS: Questions 35 through 41 are to be answered SOLELY on
              the basis of the information in the following passage.

Job evaluation and job rating systems are intended to introduce
scientific procedures. Any type of approach, when properly used,
will give satisfactory results. The Point System, when properly
validated by actual use, is more likely to be suitable for general
use than the ranking system. In many aspects, the Factor Comparison
Plan is a point system tied to money values. Of course, there may
be another system that combines the ranking system with the point
system, especially during the initial stages of the development of
the program. After the program has been in use for some time, the
tendency is to drop off the ranking phase and continue the use of
the point system.

In the ranking system of rating of jobs, every job within the plant is arranged in some order, either from the one with the simples qualifications to the one with maximum requirements, or in the revers order. This system should be preceded by careful job analysis and th writing of accurate job descriptions before the rating process is undertaken. It is possible, of course, to take the jobs as they are found in the business enterprise and use the names as they are withou any attempt at standardization, and merely rank them according to the general overall impression of the raters. Such a procedure is certai to fall short of what may reasonably be expected of job rating. Another procedure that is in reality merely a modification of the simple rating described above is to establish a series of grades or zones and arrange all the jobs in the plant into groups within these grades and zones. The practice in most common use is to arrange all the jobs in the plant according to their requirements by rating them and then to establish the classifications or groups.

The actual ranking of jobs may be done by one individual, severa individuals, or a committee. If several individuals are working independently on the task, it will usually be found that, in general, they agree but that their rankings vary in certain details. A con- ference between the individuals, with each person giving his reasons why he rated one way or another, usually produces agreement. The detailed job descriptions are particularly helpful when there is disagreement among raters as to the rating of certain jobs. It is not only possible but desirable to have workers participate in the construction of the job description and in rating the job.

35. The MAIN theme of this passage is   35.__
    A. the elimination of bias in job rating
    B. the rating of jobs by the ranking system
    C. the need for accuracy in allocating points in the
       point system
    D. pitfalls to avoid in selecting key jobs in the Factor
       Comparison Plan

36. The ranking system of rating jobs consists MAINLY of   36.__
    A. attaching a point value to each ratable factor of
       each job prior to establishing an equitable pay
       scale
    B. arranging every job in the organization in descending
       order and then following this up with a job analysis
       of the key jobs
    C. preparing accurate job descriptions after a job ana-
       lysis and then arranging all jobs either in ascending
       or descending order based on job requirements
    D. arbitrarily establishing a hierarchy of job classes
       and grades and then fitting each job into a specific
       class and grade based on the opinions of unit super-
       visors

37. The above passage states that the system of classifying   37.___
jobs MOST used in an organization is to
A. organize all jobs in the organization in accordance
with their requirements and then create categories
or clusters of jobs
B. classify all jobs in the organization according to
the titles and rank by which they are currently
known in the organization
C. establish a pre-arranged series of grades or zones
and then fit all jobs into one of the grades or zones
D. determine the salary currently being paid for each
job and then rank the jobs in order according to
salary

38. According to the above passage, experience has shown   38.___
that when a group of raters is assigned to the job
evaluation task and each individual rates independently
of the others, the raters GENERALLY
A. agree with respect to all aspects of their rankings
B. disagree with respect to all or nearly all aspects
of the rankings
C. disagree on overall ratings but agree on specific
rating factors
D. agree on overall rankings but have some variance
in some details

39. The above passage states that the use of a detailed job   39.___
description is of SPECIAL value when
A. employees of an organization have participated in
the preliminary steps involved in actual preparation of the job description
B. labor representatives are not participating in
ranking of the jobs
C. an individual rater who is unsure of himself is
ranking the jobs
D. a group of raters is having difficulty reaching
unanimity with respect to ranking a certain job

40. A comparison of the various rating systems as described   40.___
in the above passage shows that
A. the ranking system is not as appropriate for general
use as a properly validated point system
B. the point system is the same as the Factor Comparison
Plan except that it places greater emphasis on money
C. no system is capable of combining the point system
and the Factor Comparison Plan
D. the point system will be discontinued last when
used in combination with the Factor Comparison
System

41. The above passage implies that the PRINCIPAL reason for   41.___
    creating job evaluation and rating systems was to help
       A. overcome union opposition to existing salary plans
       B. base wage determination on a more objective and
          orderly foundation
       C. eliminate personal bias on the part of the trained
          scientific job evaluators
       D. management determine if it was overpricing the
          various jobs in the organizational hierarchy

42. As a general rule, in a large office it is desirable to   42.___
    have more than one employee who is able to operate any
    one machine and more than one office machine capable of
    performing any one type of required operation.
    According to this statement, there USUALLY should be
       A. fewer office machines in an office than are necessary
          for efficient job performance
       B. more office machines in an office than there are
          employees able to operate them
       C. more types of required operations to be performed
          than there are machines necessary to their perfor-
          mance
       D. fewer types of required operations to be performed
          than there are machines capable of performing them

43. The plan of an organization's structure and procedures   43.___
    may appear to be perfectly sound, but the organization
    may still operate wastefully and with a great amount of
    friction because of the failure of the people in the
    organization to work together.
    The MOST valid implication of this statement is that
       A. inefficiency within an organization may be caused
          by people being directed to do the wrong things
       B. an organization which operates inefficiently might
          be improved by revising its systems and methods of
          operations
       C. use of the best methods an organization can devise
          may not prevent an organization from being ineffi-
          cient
       D. the people in an organization may not have an appre-
          ciation of the high quality of the organization's
          plan of operations

44. If an employee is to be held responsible for obtaining   44.___
    results, he should be given every reasonable freedom to
    exercise his own intelligence and initiative to achieve
    the results expected.
    The MOST valid implication of this statement is that
       A. the authority delegated should match the responsi-
          bility assigned
       B. achieving results depends upon the individual's
          willingness to work
       C. the most important aspect of getting a job done is
          to know how to do it
       D. understanding the requirements of a task is essen-
          tial to its accomplishment

45. Essentially, an organization is defined as any group of   45.___
individuals who are cooperating under the direction of
executive leadership in an attempt to accomplish certain
common objectives.
The one of the following which this statement does NOT
include as an essential characteristic of an organization
is _____ the members of the group.
    A. cooperation among
    B. proficiency of
    C. authoritative guidance of
    D. goals common to

46. A supervisor, in organizing the work activities of the   46.___
staff of an office, should recognize that one of the
conditions which is expected to promote a high level of
interest on the part of an office worker in his job is
to assign him to perform a variety of work.
The MOST valid implication of this statement is that
    A. each worker should be taught to perform each type
       of work in the office
    B. workers should be assigned to perform types of work
       in which they have expressed interest
    C. a worker who is assigned to perform a single type
       of work is likely to become bored
    D. some workers are likely to perform several types of
       work better than other workers are able to

47. Of the following basic guides to effective letter writing, 47.___
which one would NOT be recommended as a way of improving
the quality of business letters?
    A. Use emphatic phrases like *close proximity* and *first
       and foremost* to round out sentences.
    B. Break up complicated sentences by making short
       sentences out of dependent clauses.
    C. Replace old-fashioned phrases like *enclosed please
       find* and *recent date* with a more direct approach.
    D. Personalize letters by using your reader's name at
       least once in the body of the message.

48. Suppose that you must write a reply letter to a citizen's 48.___
request for a certain pamphlet printed by your agency.
The pamphlet is temporarily unavailable but a new supply
will be arriving by December 8 or 9.
Of the following four sentences, which one expresses the
MOST positive business letter writing approach?
    A. We cannot send the materials you requested until
       after December 8.
    B. May we assure you that the materials you requested
       will be sent as quickly as possible.
    C. We will be sending the materials you requested as
       soon as our supply is replenished.
    D. We will mail the materials you requested on or
       shortly after December 8.

49. Using form letters in business correspondence is LEAST   49.___
    effective when
    A. answering letters on a frequently recurring subject
    B. giving the same information to many addresses
    C. the recipient is only interested in the routine
       information contained in the form letter
    D. a reply must be keyed to the individual require-
       ments of the intended reader

50. The ability to write memos and letters is very important   50.___
    in clerical and administrative work. Methodical planning
    of a reply letter usually involves the following basic
    steps which are arranged in random order:
    I. Determine the purpose of the letter you are about
       to write.
    II. Make an outline of what information your reply
        letter should contain.
    III. Read carefully the letter to be answered to find
         out its main points.
    IV. Assemble the facts to be included in your reply
        letter.
    V. Visualize your intended reader and adapt your letter
       writing style to him.

    If the above-numbered steps were arranged in their proper
    logical order, the one which would be THIRD in the
    sequence is
    A. II   B. III   C. IV   D. V

    _____

KEY (CORRECT ANSWERS)

1. A	11. C	21. C	31. C	41. B
2. B	12. C	22. D	32. C	42. D
3. C	13. A	23. A	33. B	43. C
4. C	14. B	24. A	34. D	44. A
5. B	15. C	25. B	35. B	45. B
6. C	16. D	26. B	36. C	46. C
7. D	17. B	27. D	37. A	47. A
8. D	18. A	28. B	38. D	48. D
9. B	19. B	29. B	39. D	49. D
10. A	20. D	30. D	40. A	50. A

_____

EXAMINATION SECTION
TEST 1

DIRECTIONS: Each question or incomplete statement is followed by several suggested answers or completions. Select the one that BEST answers the question or completes the statement. *PRINT THE LETTER OF THE CORRECT ANSWER IN THE SPACE AT THE RIGHT.*

1. In order to avoid clogging the works of a typewriter while making an erasure on a page being typed, it is BEST to
   A. remove the page from the typewriter and then erase
   B. move the carriage to the extreme right or left before you erase
   C. move the paper up until you reach the bottom of the page before you erase
   D. backspace five spaces past the error and then erase

1.____

2. In order to make the BEST use of the tabulator when typing many letters, you should set the tabulator to stop at
   A. right margin and paragraph indentation
   B. right margin and signature line
   C. center of the page and date line
   D. complimentary close and paragraph indentation

2.____

3. Suppose your supervisor is on the telephone in his office and an applicant arrives for a scheduled interview with him.
   Of the following, the BEST procedure to follow ordinarily is to
   A. informally chat with the applicant in your office until your supervisor has finished his phone conversation
   B. escort him directly into your supervisor's office and have him wait for him there
   C. inform your supervisor of the applicant's arrival and try to make the applicant feel comfortable while waiting
   D. have him hang up his coat and tell him to go directly in to see your supervisor

3.____

Questions 4-9.

DIRECTIONS: Questions 4 through 9 each consist of a sentence which may or may not be an example of good English usage. Consider grammar, punctuation, spelling, capitalization, awkwardness, etc. Examine each sentence, and then choose the correct statement about it from the four choices below it. If the English usage in the sentence given is better than any of the changes suggested in options B, C, or D, choose option A. Do not choose an option that will change the meaning of the sentence.

4. The report, along with the accompanying documents, were submitted for review.
   A. This is an example of acceptable writing.
   B. The words *were submitted* should be changed to *was submitted*.
   C. The word *accompanying* should be spelled *accompaning*.
   D. The comma after the word *report* should be taken out.

4.____

5. If others must use your files, be certain that they understand how the system works, but   5.
   insist that you do all the filing and refiling.

   A. This is an example of acceptable writing.
   B. There should be a period after the word *works*, and the word *but* should start a new
      sentence.
   C. The words *filing* and *refiling* should be spelled *fileing* and *refileing*.
   D. There should be a comma after the word *but*.

6. The appeal was not considered because of its late arrival.   6.

   A. This is an example of acceptable writing.
   B. The word *its* should be changed to *it's*.
   C. The word *its* should be changed to *the*.
   D. The words *late arrival* should be changed to *arrival late*.

7. The letter must be read carefuly to determine under which subject it should be filed.   7.

   A. This is an example of acceptable writing.
   B. The word *under* should be changed to *at*.
   C. The word *determine* should be spelled *determin*.
   D. The word *carefuly* should be spelled *carefully*.

8. He showed potential as an office manager, but he lacked skill in delegating work.   8.

   A. This is an example of acceptable writing.
   B. The word *delegating* should be spelled *delagating*.
   C. The word *potential* should be spelled *potencial*.
   D. The words *lie lacked* should be changed to *was lacking*.

9. His supervisor told him that it would be all right to receive personal mail at the office.   9

   A. This is an example of acceptable writing.
   B. The words *all right* should be changed to *alright*.
   C. The word *personal* should be spelled *personel*.
   D. The word *mail* should be changed to *letters*.

Questions 10-13.

DIRECTIONS: Questions 10 through 13 are to be answered SOLELY on the basis of the infor-
              mation given in the following passage.

*Typed pages can reflect the simplicity of modern art in a machine age. Lightness and
evenness can be achieved by proper layout and balance of typed lines and white space.
Instead of solid, cramped masses of uneven, crowded typing, there should be a pleasing balance up and down as well as horizontal.*

*To have real balance, your page must have a center. The eyes see the center of the
sheet slightly above the real center. This is the way both you and the reader see it. Try imag-
ining a line down the center of the page that divides the paper in equal halves. On either side
of your paper, white space and blocks of typing need to be similar in size and shape.
Although left and right margins should be equal, top and bottom margins need not be as
exact. It looks better to hold a bottom border wider than a top margin, so that your typing rests*

upon a cushion of white space. To add interest to the appearance of the page, try making one paragraph between one-half and two-thirds the size of an adjacent paragraph.

Thus, by taking full advantage of your typewriter, the pages that you type will not only be accurate but will also be attractive.

10. It can be inferred from the passage that the BASIC importance of proper balancing on a typed page is that proper balancing   10._____

   A. makes a typed page a work of modern art
   B. provides exercise in proper positioning of a typewriter
   C. increases the amount of typed copy on the paper
   D. draws greater attention and interest to the page

11. A reader will tend to see the center of a typed page   11._____

   A. somewhat higher than the true center
   B. somewhat lower than the true center
   C. on either side of the true center
   D. about two-thirds of an inch above the true center

12. Which of the following suggestions is NOT given by the passage?   12._____

   A. Bottom margins may be wider than top borders.
   B. Keep all paragraphs approximately the same size.
   C. Divide your page with an imaginary line down the middle.
   D. Side margins should be equalized.

13. Of the following, the BEST title for this passage is: 13._____

   A. INCREASING THE ACCURACY OF THE TYPED PAGE
   B. DETERMINATION OF MARGINS FOR TYPED COPY
   C. LAYOUT AND BALANCE OF THE TYPED PAGE
   D. HOW TO TAKE FULL ADVANTAGE OF THE TYPEWRITER

14. In order to type addresses on a large number of envelopes MOST efficiently, you should   14._____

   A. insert another envelope into the typewriter before removing each typed envelope
   B. take each typed envelope out of the machine before starting the next envelope
   C. insert several envelopes into the machine at one time, keeping all top and bottom edges even
   D. insert several envelopes into the machine at one time, keeping the top edge of each envelope two inches below the top edge of the one beneath it

15. A senior typist has completed copying a statistical report from a rough draft. Of the following, the BEST way to be sure that her typing is correct is for the typist to   15._____

   A. fold the rough draft, line it up with the typed copy, compare one-half of the columns with the original, and have a co-worker compare the other half
   B. check each line of the report as it is typed and then have a co-worker check each line again after the entire report is finished

C. have a co-worker add each column and check the totals on the typed copy with the totals on the original

D. have a co-worker read aloud from the rough draft while the typist checks the typed copy and then have the typist read while the co-worker checks

16. In order to center a heading when typing a report, you should   16.___

A. measure your typing paper with a ruler and begin the heading one-third of the way in from the left margin

B. begin the heading at the point on the typewriter scale which is 50 minus the number of letters in the heading

C. multiply the number of characters in the heading by two and begin the heading that number of spaces in from the left margin

D. begin the heading at the point on the scale which is equal to the center point of your paper minus one-half the number of characters and spaces in the heading

17. Which of the following recommendations concerning the use of copy paper for making typewritten copies should NOT be followed?   17.___

A. Copy papers should be checked for wrinkles before being used.

B. Legal-size copy paper may be folded if it is too large to fit into a convenient drawer space.

C. When several sheets of paper and carbon paper are being used, they should be fastened with a paper clip at the top after insertion in the typewriter.

D. For making many carbon copies, thin carbon paper and onionskin should be used.

18. Assume that a new typist, Norma Garcia, has been assigned to work under your supervision and is reporting to work for the first time. You formally introduce Norma to her co-workers and suggest that a few of the other typists explain the office procedures and typing formats to her. The practice of instructing Norma in her duties in this manner is   18.___

A. *good* because she will be made to feel at home

B. *good* because she will learn more about routine office tasks from co-workers than from you

C. *poor* because her co-workers will resent the extra work

D. *poor* because you will not have enough control over her training

19. Suppose that Jean Brown, a typist, is typing a letter following the same format that she has always used. However, she notices that the other two typists in her office are also typing letters, but are using a different format. Jean is concerned that she might not have been informed of a change in format.   19

Of the following, the FIRST action that Jean should take is to

A. seek advice from her supervisor as to which format to use

B. ask the other typists whether she should use a new format for typing letters

C. disregard the format that the other typists are using and continue to type in the format she had been using

D. use the format that the other typists are using, assuming that it is a newly accepted method

20. Suppose that the new office to which you have been assigned has put up Christmas dec- 20.____
    orations, and a Christmas party is being planned by the city agency in which you work.
    However, nothing has been said about Christmas gifts.
    It would be CORRECT for you to assume that

    A. you are expected to give a gift to your supervisor
    B. your supervisor will give you a gift
    C. you are expected to give gifts only to your subordinates
    D. you will neither receive gifts nor will you be expected to give any

———

KEY (CORRECT ANSWERS)

1.	B	11.	A
2.	D	12.	B
3.	C	13.	C
4.	B	14.	A
5.	A	15.	D
6.	A	16.	D
7.	D	17.	B
8.	A	18.	D
9.	A	19.	A
10.	D	20.	D

———

TEST 2

Each question or incomplete statement is followed by several suggested answers or completions. Select the one that BEST answers the question or completes the statement. *PRINT THE LETTER OF THE CORRECT ANSWER IN THE SPACE AT THE RIGHT.*

1. The supervisor you assist is under great pressure to meet certain target dates. He has   1.
    scheduled an emergency meeting to take place in a few days, and he asks you to send
    out notices immediately. As you begin to prepare the notices, however, you realize he
    has scheduled the meeting for a Saturday, which is not a working day. Also, you sense
    that your supervisor is not in a good mood.
    Which of the following is the MOST effective method of handling this situation?

    A. Change the meeting date to the first working day after that Saturday and send out
        the notices.
    B. Change the meeting date to a working day on which his calendar is clear and send
        out the notices.
    C. Point out to your supervisor that the date is a Saturday.
    D. Send out the notices as they are since you have received specific instructions.

Questions 2-7.

DIRECTIONS: Questions 2 through 7 each consist of a sentence which may or may not be an
              example of good English usage. Consider grammar, punctuation, spelling,
              capitalization, awkwardness, etc. Examine each sentence, and then choose
              the correct statement about it from the four choices below it. If the English
              usage in the sentence given is better than any of the changes suggested in
              options B, C, or D, choose option A. Do not choose an option that will change
              the meaning of the sentence.

2. The typist used an extention cord in order to connect her typewriter to the outlet nearest   2
    to her desk.

    A. This is an example of acceptable writing.
    B. A period should be placed after the word *cord,* and the word *in* should have a capi-
        tal *I.*
    C. A comma should be placed after the word *typewriter.*
    D. The word *extention* should be spelled *extension.*

3. He would have went to the conference if he had received an invitation.   3

    A. This is an example of acceptable writing.
    B. The word *went* should be replaced by the word *gone.*
    C. The word *had* should be replaced by *would have.*
    D. The word *conference* should be spelled *conferance.*

4. In order to make the report neater, he spent many hours rewriting it.

    A. This is an example of acceptable writing.
    B. The word *more* should be inserted before the word *neater.*
    C. There should be a colon after the word *neater.*
    D. The word *spent* should be changed to *have spent.*

5. His supervisor told him that he should of read the memorandum more carefully.   5._____

    A. This is an example of acceptable writing.
    B. The word *memorandum* should be spelled *memorandom*.
    C. The word *of* should be replaced by the word *have*.
    D. The word *carefully* should be replaced by the word *careful*.

6. It was decided that two separate reports should be written.   6._____

    A. This is an example of acceptable writing.
    B. A comma should be inserted after the word *decided*.
    C. The word *be* should be replaced by the word *been*.
    D. A colon should be inserted after the word *that*.

7. She don't seem to understand that the work must be done as soon as possible.   7._____

    A. This is an example of acceptable writing.
    B. The word *doesn't* should replace the word *don't*.
    C. The word *why* should replace the word *that*.
    D. The word *as* before the word *soon* should be eliminated.

Questions 8-11.

DIRECTIONS: Questions 8 through 11 are to be answered SOLELY on the basis of the following passage.

There is nothing that will take the place of good sense on the part of the stenographer. You may be perfect in transcribing exactly what the dictator says and your speed may be adequate; but without an understanding of the dictator's intent as well as his words, you are likely to be a mediocre secretary.

A serious error that is made when taking dictation is putting down something that does not make sense. Most people who dictate material would rather be asked to repeat and explain than to receive transcribed material which has errors due to inattention or doubt. Many dictators request that their grammar be corrected by their secretaries; but unless specifically asked to do so, secretaries should not do it without first checking with the dictator. Secretaries should be aware that, in some cases, dictators may use incorrect grammar or slang expressions to create a particular effect.

Some people dictate commas, periods, and paragraphs, while others expect the stenographer to know when, where, and how to punctuate. A well-trained secretary should be able to indicate the proper punctuation by listening to the pauses and tones of the dictator's voice.

A stenographer who has taken dictation from the same person for a period of time should be able to understand him under most conditions. By increasing her tact, alertness, and efficiency, a secretary can become more competent.

8. According to the passage, which of the following statements concerning the dictation of punctuation is CORRECT?   8._____
  A

    A. dictator may use incorrect punctuation to create a desired style

B. dictator should indicate all punctuation

C. stenographer should know how to punctuate based on the pauses and tones of the dictator

D. stenographer should not type any punctuation if it has not been dictated to her

9. According to the passage, how should secretaries handle grammatical errors in a dictation?
Secretaries should

A. *not correct* grammatical errors unless the dictator is aware that this is being done

B. *correct* grammatical errors by having the dictator repeat the line with proper pauses

C. *correct* grammatical errors if they have checked the correctness in a grammar book

D. *correct* grammatical errors based on their own good sense

10. If a stenographer is confused about the method of spacing and indenting of a report which has just been dictated to her, she GENERALLY should

A. do the best she can

B. ask the dictator to explain what she should do

C. try to improve her ability to understand dictated material

D. accept the fact that her stenographic ability is not adequate

11. In the last line of the first paragraph, the word *mediocre* means MOST NEARLY

A. superior   B. disregarded
C. respected   D. second-rate

12. Assume that is is your responsibility to schedule meetings for your supervisor, who believes in starting these meetings strictly on time. He has told you to schedule separate meetings with Mr. Smith and Ms. Jones, which will last approximately 20 minutes each. You have told Mr. Smith to arrive at 10:00 A.M. and Ms. Jones at 10:30 A.M. Your supervisor will have an hour of free time at 11:00 A.M. At 10:25 A.M., Mr. Smith arrives and states that there was a train delay, and he is sorry that he is late. Ms. Jones has not yet arrived. You do not know who Mr. Smith and Ms. Jones are or what the meetings will be about.
Of the following, the BEST course of action for you to take is to

A. send Mr. Smith in to see your supervisor; and when Ms. Jones arrives, tell her that your supervisor's first meeting will take more time than he expected

B. tell Mr. Smith that your supervisor has a meeting at 10:30 A.M. and that you will have to reschedule his meeting for another day

C. check with your supervisor to find out if he would prefer to see Mr. Smith immediately or at 11:00 A.M.

D. encourage your supervisor to meet with Mr. Smith immediately because Mr. Smith's late arrival was not intentional

13. Assume that you have been told by your boss not to let anyone disturb him for the rest of the afternoon unless absolutely necessary since he has to complete some urgent work. His supervisor, who is the bureau chief, telephones and asks to speak to him.
The BEST course of action for you to take is to

A. ask the bureau chief if he can leave a message
B. ask your boss if he can take the call
C. tell the bureau chief that your boss is out
D. tell your boss that his instructions will get you into trouble

14. Which one of the following is the MOST advisable procedure for a stenographer to follow when a dictator asks her to make extra copies of dictated material?   14.____

    A. Note the number of copies required at the beginning of the notes.
    B. Note the number of copies required at the end of the notes.
    C. Make a mental note of the number of copies required to be made.
    D. Make a checkmark beside the notes to serve as a reminder that extra copies are required.

15. Suppose that, as you are taking shorthand notes, the dictator tells you that the sentence he has just dictated is to be deleted.   15.____
Of the following, the BEST thing for you to do is to

    A. place the correction in the left-hand margin next to the deleted sentence
    B. write the word *delete* over the sentence and place the correction on a separate page for corrections
    C. erase the sentence and use that available space for the correction
    D. draw a line through the sentence and begin the correction on the next available line

16. Assume that your supervisor, who normally dictates at a relatively slow rate, begins dictating to you very rapidly. You find it very difficult to keep up at this speed. Which one of the following is the BEST action to take in this situation?   16.____

    A. Ask your supervisor to dictate more slowly since you are having difficulty.
    B. Continue to take the dictation at the fast speed and fill in the blanks later.
    C. Interrupt your supervisor with a question about the dictation, hoping that when she begins again it will be slower.
    D. Refuse to take the dictation unless given at the speed indicated in your job description.

17. Assume that you have been asked to put a heading on the second, third, and fourth pages of a four-page letter to make sure they can be identified in case they are separated from the first page.   17.____
Which of the following is it LEAST important to include in such a heading?

    A. Date of the letter
    B. Initials of the typist
    C. Name of the person to whom the letter is addressed
    D. Number of the page

18. Which one of the following is NOT generally accepted when dividing words at the end of a line?   18.____
Dividing

    A. a hyphenated word at the hyphen
    B. a word immediately after the prefix
    C. a word immediately before the suffix
    D. proper names between syllables

19. In the preparation of a business letter which has two enclosures, the MOST generally accepted of the following procedures to follow is to type

    A. *See Attached Items* one line below the last line of the body of the letter
    B. *See Attached Enclosures* to the left of the signature
    C. *Enclosures 2* at the left margin below the signature line
    D. nothing on the letter to indicate enclosures since it will be obvious to the reader that there are enclosures in the envelope

19.

20. Standard rules for typing spacing have developed through usage. According to these rules, one space is left AFTER

    A. a comma   B. every sentence
    C. a colon   D. an opening parenthesis

20.

KEY (CORRECT ANSWERS)

1.	C	11.	D
2.	D	12.	C
3.	B	13.	B
4.	A	14.	A
5.	C	15.	D
6.	A	16.	A
7.	B	17.	B
8.	C	18.	D
9.	A	19.	C
10.	B	20.	A

EXAMINATION SECTION
TEST 1

DIRECTIONS: Each question or incomplete statement is followed by several suggested answers or completions. Select the one that BEST answers the question or completes the statement. *PRINT THE LETTER OF THE CORRECT ANSWER IN THE SPACE AT THE RIGHT.*

1. A push-button telephone with six buttons, one of which is a *hold* button, is often used when more than one outside line is needed.
   If you are talking on one line of this type of telephone when another call comes in, what is the procedure to follow if you want to answer the second call but keep the first call on the line? Push the   1.____

   A. *hold* button at the same time as you push the *pickup* button of the ringing line
   B. *hold* button and then push the *pickup* button of the ringing line
   C. *pickup* button of the ringing line and then push the *hold* button
   D. *pickup* button of the ringing line and push the *hold* button when you return to the original line

2. Suppose that you are asked to prepare a petty cash statement for March. The original and one copy are to go to the personnel office. One copy is to go to the fiscal office, and another copy is to go to your supervisor. The last copy is for your files.
   In preparing the statement and the copies, how many sheets of copy paper should you use?   2.____

   A. 3   B. 4   C. 5   D. 8

3. Which one of the following is the LEAST important advantage of putting the subject of a letter in the heading to the right of the address?   3.____
   It

   A. makes filing of the copy ea.sier
   B. makes more space available in the body of the letter
   C. simplifies distribution of letters
   D. simplifies determination of the subject of the letter

4. Of the following, the MOST efficient way to put 100 copies of a one-page letter into 9 1/2" x 4 1/8" envelopes for mailing is to fold _____ into an envelope.   4.____

   A. each letter and insert it immediately after folding
   B. each letter separately until all 100 are folded; then insert each one
   C. the 100 letters two at a time, then separate them and insert each one
   D. two letters together, slip them apart, and insert each one

5. When preparing papers for filing, it is NOT desirable to   5.____

   A. smooth papers that are wrinkled
   B. use paper clips to keep related papers together in the files
   C. arrange the papers in the order in which they will be filed
   D. mend torn papers with cellophane tape

6. Of the following, the BEST reason for a clerical unit to have its own duplicating machine is that the unit   6.___

    A. uses many forms which it must reproduce internally
    B. must make two copies of each piece of incoming mail for a special file
    C. must make seven copies of each piece of outgoing mail
    D. must type 200 envelopes each month for distribution to the same offices

7. Several offices use the same photocopying machine.   7.___
If each office must pay its share of the cost of running this machine, the BEST way of determining how much of this cost should be charged to each of these offices is to

    A. determine the monthly number of photocopies made by each office
    B. determine the monthly number of originals submitted for photocopying by each office
    C. determine the number of times per day each office uses the photocopy machine
    D. divide the total cost of running the photocopy machine by the total number of offices using the machine

8. Which one of the following would it be BEST to use to indicate that a file folder has been removed from the files for temporary use in another office?   8.___
A(n)

    A. cross-reference card   B. tickler file marker
    C. aperture card   D. out guide

9. Which one of the following is the MOST important objective of filing?   9

    A. Giving a secretary something to do in her spare time
    B. Making it possible to locate information quickly
    C. Providing a place to store unneeded documents
    D. Keeping extra papers from accumulating on workers' desks

10. If a check has been made out for an incorrect amount, the BEST action for the writer of the check to take is to   10

    A. erase the original amount and enter the correct amount
    B. cross out the original amount with a single line and enter the correct amount above it
    C. black out the original amount so that it cannot be read and enter the correct amount above it
    D. write a new check

11. Which one of the following BEST describes the usual arrangement of a tickler file?   11

    A. Alphabetical   B. Chronological
    C. Numerical   D. Geographical

12. Which one of the following is the LEAST desirable filing practice?   12

    A. Using staples to keep papers together
    B. Filing all material without regard to date
    C. Keeping a record of all materials removed from the files
    D. Writing filing instructions on each paper prior to filing

13. Assume that one of your duties is to keep records of the office supplies used by your unit   13.____
    for the purpose of ordering new supplies when the old supplies run out. The information
    that will be of MOST help in letting you know when to reorder supplies is the

    A. quantity issued   B. quantity received
    C. quantity on hand   D. stock number

Questions 14-19.

DIRECTIONS: Questions 14 through 19 consist of sets of names and addresses. In each
              question, the name and address in Column II should be an exact copy of the
              name and address in Column I. If there is:
                  a mistake *only* in the name, mark your answer A;
                  a mistake *only* in the address, mark your answer B;
                  a mistake in *both* name and address, mark your answer C;
                  no mistake in *either* name or address, mark your answer D.

SAMPLE QUESTION

Column I   Column II
Michael Filbert   Michael Filbert
456 Reade Street   645 Reade Street
New York, N.Y. 10013   New York, N.Y. 10013

Since there is a mistake only in the address (the street number should be 456
instead of 645), the answer to the sample question is B.

COLUMN I   COLUMN II

14. Esta Wong   Esta Wang   14.____
    141 West 68 St.   141 West 68 St.
    New York, N.Y. 10023   New York, N.Y. 10023

15. Dr. Alberto Grosso   Dr. Alberto Grosso   15.____
    3475 12th Avenue   3475 12th Avenue
    Brooklyn, N.Y. 11218   Brooklyn, N.Y. 11218

16. Mrs. Ruth Bortlas   Ms. Ruth Bortlas   16.____
    482 Theresa Ct.   482 Theresa Ct.
    Far Rockaway, N.Y. 11691   Far Rockaway, N.Y. 11169

17. Mr. and Mrs. Howard Fox   Mr. and Mrs. Howard Fox   17.____
    2301 Sedgwick Ave.   231 Sedgwick Ave.
    Bronx, N.Y. 10468   Bronx, N.Y. 10468

18. Miss Marjorie Black   Miss Margorie Black   18.____
    223 East 23 Street   223 East 23 Street
    New York, N.Y. 10010   New York, N.Y. 10010

19. Michelle Herman   Michelle Hermann   19.____
    806 Valley Rd.   806 Valley Dr.
    Old Tappan, N.J. 07675   Old Tappan, N.J. 07675

Questions 20-25.

DIRECTIONS: Questions 20 through 25 are to be answered SOLELY on the basis of the information in the following passage.

Basic to every office is the need for proper lighting. Inadequate lighting is a familiar cause
of fatigue and serves to create a somewhat dismal atmosphere in the office. One requirement
of proper lighting is that it be of an appropriate intensity. Intensity is measured in foot-candles.
According to the Illuminating Engineering Society of New York, for casual seeing tasks such
as in reception rooms, inactive file rooms, and other service areas, it is recommended that
the amount of light be 30 foot-candles. For ordinary seeing tasks such as reading and work in
active file rooms and in mail rooms, the recommended lighting is 100 foot-candles. For very
difficult seeing tasks such as accounting, transcribing, and business machine use, the recommended lighting is 150 foot-candles.

Lighting intensity is only one requirement. Shadows and glare are to be avoided. For
example, the larger the proportion of a ceiling filled with lighting units, the more glare-free and
comfortable the lighting will be. Natural lighting from windows is not too dependable because
on dark wintry days, windows yield little usable light, and on sunny, summer afternoons, the
glare from windows may be very distracting. Desks should not face the windows. Finally, the
main lighting source ought to be overhead and to the left of the user.

20.   According to the above passage, insufficient light in the office may cause   20.___

   A.   glare   B.   shadows
   C.   tiredness   D.   distraction

21.   Based on the above passage, which of the following must be considered when planning   21.___
       lighting arrangements?
       The

   A.   amount of natural light present
   B.   amount of work to be done
   C.   level of difficulty of work to be done
   D.   type of activity to be carried out

22.   It can be inferred from the above passage that a well-coordinated lighting scheme is   22.___
       LIKELY to result in

   A.   greater employee productivity
   B.   elimination of light reflection
   C.   lower lighting cost
   D.   more use of natural light

23.   Of the following, the BEST title for the above passage is   23.___

   A.   Characteristics of Light
   B.   Light Measurement Devices
   C.   Factors to Consider When Planning Lighting Systems
   D.   Comfort vs. Cost When Devising Lighting Arrangements

24. According to the above passage, a foot-candle is a measurement of the

    A. number of bulbs used
    B. strength of the light
    C. contrast between glare and shadow
    D. proportion of the ceiling filled with lighting units

24.____

25. According to the above passage, the number of foot-candles of light that would be needed to copy figures onto a payroll is _____ foot-candles.

    A. less than 30   B. 30
    C. 100   D. 150

25.____

KEY (CORRECT ANSWERS)

1.	B	11.	B
2.	B	12.	B
3.	B	13.	C
4.	A	14.	A
5.	B	15.	D
6.	A	16.	C
7.	A	17.	B
8.	D	18.	A
9.	B	19.	C
10.	D	20.	C

21.	D
22.	A
23.	C
24.	B
25.	D

TEST 2

DIRECTIONS: Each question or incomplete statement is followed by several suggested answers or completions. Select the one that BEST answers the question or completes the statement. *PRINT THE LETTER OF THE CORRECT ANSWER IN THE SPACE AT THE RIGHT.*

1. Assume that a supervisor has three subordinates who perform clerical tasks. One of the employees retires and is replaced by someone who is transferred from another unit in the agency. The transferred employee tells the supervisor that she has worked as a clerical employee for two years and understands clerical operations quite well. The supervisor then assigns the transferred employee to a desk, tells the employee to begin working, and returns to his own desk.
The supervisor's action in this situation is   1.

   A. *proper;* experienced clerical employees do not require training when they are transferred to new assignments
   B. *improper;* before the supervisor returns to his desk, he should tell the other two subordinates to watch the transferred employee perform the work
   C. *proper;* if the transferred employee makes any mistakes, she will bring them to the supervisor's attention
   D. *improper;* the supervisor should find out what clerical tasks the transferred employee has performed and give her instruction in those which are new or different

2. Assume that you are falling behind in completing your work assignments and you believe that your workload is too heavy.
Of the following, the BEST course of action for you to take FIRST is to   2

   A. discuss the problem with your supervisor
   B. decide which of your assignments can be postponed
   C. try to get some of your co-workers to help you out
   D. plan to take some of the work home with you in order to catch up

3. Suppose that one of the clerks under your supervision is filling in monthly personnel forms. She asks you to explain a particular personnel regulation which is related to various items on the forms. You are not thoroughly familiar with the regulation.
Of the following responses you may make, the one which will gain the MOST respect from the clerk and which is generally the MOST advisable is to   3

   A. tell the clerk to do the best she can and that you will check her work later
   B. inform the clerk that you are not sure of a correct explanation but suggest a procedure for her to follow
   C. give the clerk a suitable interpretation so that she will think you are familiar with all regulations
   D. tell the clerk that you will have to read the regulation more thoroughly before you can give her an explanation

4. Charging out records until a specified due date, with prompt follow-up if they are not returned, is a   4

A. *good* idea; it may prevent the records from being kept needlessly on someone's desk for long periods of time
B. *good* idea; it will indicate the extent of your authority to other departments
C. *poor* idea; the person borrowing the material may make an error because of the pressure put upon him to return the records
D. *poor* idea; other departments will feel that you do not trust them with the records and they will be resentful

Questions 5-9.

DIRECTIONS: Questions 5 through 9 consist of three lines of code letters and numbers. The numbers on each line should correspond with the code letters on the same line in accordance with the table below.

Code Letter	P	L	I	J	B	0	H	U	C	G
Corresponding Number	0	1	2	3	4	5	6	7	8	9

On some of the lines, an error exists in the coding. Compare the letters and numbers in each question carefully. If you find an error or errors on
   only *one* of the lines in the question, mark your answer A;
   any *two* lines in the question, mark your answer B;
   all *three* lines in the question, mark your answer C;
   none of the lines in the question, mark your answer D.

SAMPLE QUESTION

JHOILCP   3652180
BICLGUP   4286970
UCIBHLJ   5824613

In the above sample, the first line is correct since each code letter listed has the correct corresponding number. On the second line, an error exists because code letter L should have the number 1 instead of the number 6. On the third line, an error exists because the code letter U should have the number 7 instead of the number 5. Since there are errors on two of the three lines, the correct answer is B.

5. BULJCIP   4713920   5._____
   HIGPOUL   6290571
   OCUHJBI   5876342

6. CUBLOIJ   8741023   6._____
   LCLGCLB   1818914
   JPUHIOC   3076158

7. OIJGCBPO   52398405   7._____
   UHPBLIOP   76041250
   CLUIPGPC   81720908

8. BPCOUOJI   40875732   8.
    UOHCIPLB   75682014
    GLHUUCBJ   92677843

9. HOIOHJLH   65256361   9.
    IOJJHHBP   25536640
    OJHBJOPI   53642502

Questions 10-13.

DIRECTIONS: Questions 10 through 13 are to be answered SOLELY on the basis of the information given in the following passage.

The mental attitude of the employee toward safety is exceedingly important in preventing accidents. All efforts designed to keep safety on the employee's mind and to keep accident prevention a live subject in the office will help substantially in a safety program. Although it may seem strange, it is common for people to be careless. Therefore, safety education is a continuous process.

Safety rules should be explained, and the reasons for their rigid enforcement should be given to employees. Telling employees to be careful or giving similar general safety warnings and slogans is probably of little value. Employees should be informed of basic safety fundamentals. This can be done through staff meetings, informal suggestions to employees, movies, and safety instruction cards. Safety instruction cards provide the employees with specific suggestions about safety and serve as a series of timely reminders helping to keep safety on the minds of employees. Pictures, posters, and cartoon sketches on bulletin boards that are located in areas continually used by employees arouse the employees' interest in safety. It is usually good to supplement this type of safety promotion with intensive individual follow-up.

10. The above passage implies that the LEAST effective of the following safety measures is   10

     A.   rigid enforcement of safety rules
     B.   getting employees to think in terms of safety
     C.   elimination of unsafe conditions in the office
     D.   telling employees to stay alert at all times

11. The reason given by the passage for maintaining ongoing safety education is that   11

     A.   people are often careless
     B.   office tasks are often dangerous
     C.   the value of safety slogans increases with repetition
     D.   safety rules change frequently

12. Which one of the following safety aids is MOST likely to be preferred by the passage?   12
    A

     A.   cartoon of a man tripping over a carton and yelling, *Keep aisles clear!*
     B.   poster with a large number one and a caption saying, *Safety First*
     C.   photograph of a very neatly arranged office
     D.   large sign with the word *THINK* in capital letters

13. Of the following, the BEST title for the above passage is   13.____

    A. Basic Safety Fundamentals
    B. Enforcing Safety Among Careless Employees
    C. Attitudes Toward Safety
    D. Making Employees Aware of Safety

Questions 14-21.

DIRECTIONS: Questions 14 through 21 are to be answered SOLELY on the basis of the infor-
                mation and the chart given below.

    The following chart shows expenses in five selected categories for a one-year period, expressed as percentages of these same expenses during the previous year. The chart compares two different offices. In Office T (represented by ▨), a cost reduction program has been tested for the past year. The other office, Office Q (represented by ▨), served as a control, in that no special effort was made' to reduce costs during the past year.

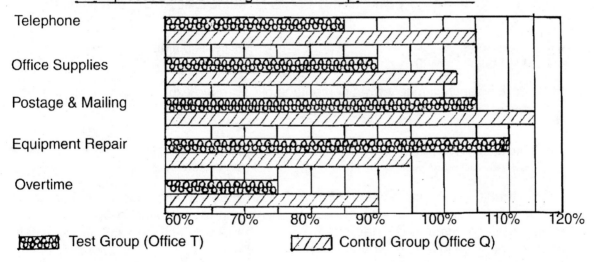

RESULTS OF OFFICE COST REDUCTION PROGRAM

Expenses of Test and Control Groups for 1999
Expressed as Percentages of Same Expenses for 1998

▨ Test Group (Office T)   ▨ Control Group (Office Q)

14. In Office T, which category of expense showed the greatest percentage REDUCTION   14.____
from 1998 to 1999?

    A. Telephone   B. Office Supplies
    C. Postage & Mailing   D. Overtime

15. In which expense category did Office T show the BEST results in percentage terms   15.____
when compared to Office Q?

    A. Telephone   B. Office Supplies
    C. Postage & Mailing   D. Overtime

16. According to the above chart, the cost reduction program was LEAST effective for the   16.
    expense category of

    A. Office Supplies   B. Postage & Mailing
    C. Equipment Repair   D. Overtime

17. Office T's telephone costs went down during 1999 by approximately how many percent-   17.
    age points?

    A. 15   B. 20   C. 85   D. 105

18. Which of the following changes occurred in expenses for Office Supplies in Office Q in   18.
    the year 1999 as compared with the year 1998 ?
    They

    A. increased by more than 100%
    B. remained the same
    C. decreased by a few percentage points
    D. increased by a few percentage points

19. For which of the following expense categories do the results in Office T and the results in   19.
    Office Q differ MOST NEARLY by 10 percentage points?

    A. Telephone   B. Postage & Mailing
    C. Equipment Repair   D. Overtime

20. In which expense category did Office Q's costs show the GREATEST percentage   20
    increase in 1999?

    A. Telephone   B. Office Supplies
    C. Postage & Mailing   D. Equipment Repair

21. In Office T, by approximately what percentage did overtime expense change during the   21
    past year?
    It

    A. increased by 15%   B. increased by 75%
    C. decreased by 10%   D. decreased by 25%

22. In a particular agency, there were 160 accidents in 1997. Of these accidents, 75% were   22
    due to unsafe acts and the rest were due to unsafe conditions. In the following year, a
    special safety program was established. The number of accidents in 1999 due to unsafe
    acts was reduced to 35% of what it had been in 1997-
    How many accidents due to unsafe acts were there in 1999?

    A. 20   B. 36   C. 42   D. 56

23. At the end of every month, the petty cash fund of Agency A is reimbursed for payments   23
    made from the fund during the month. During the month of February, the amounts paid
    from the fund were entered on receipts as follows: 10 bus fares of 35¢ each and one taxi
    fare of $3.50.
    At the end of the month, the money left in the fund was in the following denominations:
    15 one dollar bills, 4 quarters, 10 dimes, and 20 nickels.
    If the petty cash fund is reduced by 20% for the following month, how much money will
    there be available in the petty cash fund for March?

    A. $11.00   B. $20.00   C. $21.50   D. $25.00

24. The one of the following records which it would be MOST advisable to keep in alphabeti- 24._____
cal order is a

    A. continuous listing of phone messages, including time and caller, for your supervi-
sor
    B. listing of individuals currently employed by your agency in a particular title
    C. record of purchases paid for by the petty cash fund
    D. dated record of employees who have borrowed material from the files in your office

25. Assume that you have been asked to copy by hand a column of numbers with two deci- 25._____
mal places from one record to another. Each number consists of three, four, and five digits.
In order to copy them quickly and accurately, you should copy

    A. each number exactly, making sure that the column of digits farthest to the right is in
a straight line and all other columns are lined up
    B. the column of digits farthest to the right and then copy the next column of digits
moving from right to left
    C. the column of digits farthest to the left and then copy the next column of digits mov-
ing from left to right
    D. the digits to the right of each decimal point and then copy the digits to the left of
each decimal point

KEY (CORRECT ANSWERS)

1.	D		11.	A
2.	A		12.	A
3.	D		13.	D
4.	A		14.	D
5.	A		15.	A
6.	C		16.	C
7.	D		17.	A
8.	B		18.	D
9.	C		19.	B
10.	D		20.	C

21. D
22. C
23. B
24. B
25. A

EXAMINATION SECTION
TEST 1

DIRECTIONS: Each question or incomplete statement is followed by several suggested answers or completions. Select the one that BEST answers the question or completes the statement. *PRINT THE LETTER OF THE CORRECT ANSWER IN THE SPACE AT THE RIGHT.*

Questions 1-2.

DIRECTIONS: Questions 1 and 2 are to be answered on the basis of the following conditions.

Assume that you work for Department A, which occupies several floors in one building. There is a reception office on each floor. All visitors (persons not employed in the department) are required to go to the reception office on the same floor as the office of the person they want to see. They sign a register, their presence is announced by the receptionist, and they wait in the reception room for the person they are visiting.

1. As you are walking in the corridor of your department on your way to a meeting in Room 314, a visitor approaches you and asks you to direct her to Room 312. She says that she is delivering some papers to Mr. Crane in that office. The MOST APPROPRIATE action for you to take is to

   A. offer to deliver the papers to Mr. Crane since you will be passing his office
   B. suggest that she come with you since you will be passing Room 312
   C. direct her to the reception office where Mr. Crane will be contacted for her
   D. take her to the reception office and contact Mr. Crane for her

1._____

2. You are acting as receptionist in the reception office on the second floor. A man enters, stating that he is an accountant from another department and that he has an appointment with Mr. Prince, who is located in Room 102 on the first floor.
The BEST action for you to take is to

   A. phone the reception office on the first floor and ask the receptionist to contact Mr. Prince
   B. advise the man to go to the reception office on the first floor where he will be further assisted
   C. contact Mr. Prince for him and ask that he come to your office where his visitor is waiting
   D. send him directly to Room 102 where he can see Mr. Prince

2._____

3. One of the employees whom you supervise complains to you that you give her more work than the other employees and that she cannot finish these assignments by the time you expect them to be completed.
Of the following, the FIRST action you should then take is to

   A. tell the employee that you expect more work from her because the other employees do not have her capabilities
   B. assure the employee that you always divide the work equally among your subordinates

3._____

  C. review the employee's recent assignments in order to determine whether her complaint is justified

  D. ask the employee if there are any personal problems which are interfering with the completion of the assignments

4. Assume that a staff regulation exists which requires an employee to inform his supervisor if the employee will be absent on a particular day.
  If an employee fails to follow this regulation, the FIRST action his supervisor should take is to

  A. inform his own supervisor of the situation and ask for further instructions
  B. ask the employee to explain his failure to follow the regulation
  C. tell the employee that another breach of the regulation will lead to disciplinary action
  D. reprimand the employee for failing to follow the regulation

                      4._

5. An employee tells his supervisor that he submitted an idea to the employees' suggestion program by mail over two months ago and still has not received an indication that the suggestion is being considered. The employee states that when one of his co-workers sent in a suggestion, he received a response within one week. The employee then asks his supervisor what he should do.
  Which of the following is the BEST response for the supervisor to make?

  A. "Next time you have a suggestion, see me about it first and I will make sure that it is properly handled."
  B. "I'll try to find out whether your suggestion was received by the program and whether a response was sent."
  C. "Your suggestion probably wasn't that good so there's no sense in pursuing the matter any further."
  D. "Let's get together and submit the suggestion jointly so that it will carry more weight."

                      5._

6. Assume that you have been trying to teach a newly appointed employee the filing procedures used in your office. The employee seems to be having difficulty learning the procedures even though you consider them relatively simple and you originally learned them in less time than you have already spent trying to teach the new employee.
  Before you spend any time trying to teach him any new filing procedures, which of the following actions should you take FIRST?

  A. Try to teach him some other aspect of your office's work.
  B. Tell him that you had little difficulty learning the procedures and ask him why he finds them so hard to learn.
  C. Review with him those procedures you have tried to teach him and determine whether he understands them.
  D. Report to your supervisor that the new employee is unsuited for the work performed in your office.

                      6.

7. There is a rule in your office that all employees must sign in and out for lunch. You notice that a new employee who is under your direct supervision has not signed in or out for lunch for the past three days. Of the following, the MOST effective action to take is to

                      7

A.   immediately report this matter to your supervisor
B.   note this infraction of rules on the employee's personnel record
C.   remind the employee that she must sign in and out for lunch every day
D.   send around a memorandum to all employees in the office telling them they must sign in and out for lunch every day

Questions 8-15.

DIRECTIONS: Questions 8 through 15 each show in Column I names written on four cards (lettered w, x, y, z) which have to be filed. You are to choose the option (lettered A, B, C, or D) in Column II which BEST represents the proper order of filing according to the rules and sample question given below. The cards are to be filed according to the following Rules for Alphabetical Filing.

RULES FOR ALPHABETICAL FILING

Names of Individuals

1.   *The names of individuals are filed in strict alphabetical order, first according to the last name, then according to first name or initial, and finally according to middle name or initial. For example: George Allen precedes Edward Bell and Leonard Reston precedes Lucille Reston.*

2.   *When last names are the same, for example, A. Green and Agnes Green, the one with the initial comes before the one with the name written out when the first initials are identical.*

3.   *When first and last names are the same, a name without a middle initial comes before one with a middle initial. For example: Ralph Simon comes before both Ralph A. Simon and Ralph Adam Simon.*

4.   *When first and last names are the same, a name with a middle initial comes before one with a middle name beginning with the same initial. For example: Sam P. Rogers comes before Sam Paul Rogers.*

5.   *Prefixes such as De , 0', Mac, Mc, and Van are filed as written and are treated as part of the names to which they are connected. For example: Gladys McTeaque is filed before Frances Meadows.*

6.   *Abbreviated names are treated as if they were spelled out. For example: Chas. is filed as Charles and Thos. is filed as Thomas.*

7.   *Titles and designations such as Dr., Mr., and Prof, are ignored in filing.*

Names of Organizations

1.   *The names of business organizations are filed according to the order in which each word in the name appears. When an organization name bears the name of a person, it is filed according to the rules for filing names of people as given above. Vivian Quinn Boutique would, therefore, come before Security Locks Inc. because Quinn comes before Security.*

2. When numerals occur in a name, they are treated as if they were spelled out. For example: 4th Street Thrift Shop is filed as Fourth Street Thrift Shop.

3. When the following words are part of the name of an organization, they are ignored: on, the, of, and.

SAMPLE

	Column I	Column II	The correct way to file the cards is:
w.	Jane Earl	A. w, y, z, x	y. James Earl
x.	James A. Earle	B. y, w, z, x	w. Jane Earl
y.	James Earl	C. x, y, w, z	z. J. Earle
z.	J. Earle	D. x, w, y, z	x. James A. Earle

The correct filing order is shown by the letters, y, w, z, x (in that sequence). Since, in Column II, B appears in front of the letters, y, w, z, x (in that sequence), B is the correct answer to the sample question.

Now answer the following questions using that same procedure.

Column I   **Column II**

8.
w. James Rothschild
x. Julius B. Rothchild
y. B. Rothstein
z. Brian Joel Rothenstein

A. x, z, w, y
B. x, w, z, y
C. z, y, w, x
D. z, w, x, y

9.
w. George S. Wise
x. S. G. Wise
y. Geo. Stuart Wise
z. Prof. Diana Wise

A. w, y, z, x
B. x , w , y , z
C. y, x, w, z
D. z, w, y, x

10.
w. 10th Street Bus Terminal
x. Buckingham Travel Agency
y. The Buckingham Theater
z. Burt Tompkins Studio

A. x, z, w, y
B. y, x, w, z
C. w, z, y, x
D. x, w, y, z

11.
w. National Council of American Importers
x. National Chain Co. of Providence
y. National Council on Alcoholism
z. National Chain Co.

A. w, y, x, z
B. x, z, w, y
C. z, x, w, y
D. z, x, y, w

12.
w. Dr. Herbert Alvary
x. Mr. Victor Alvarado
y. Alvar Industries
z. V. Alvarado

A. w, y, x, z
B. z, w, x, y
C. y, z, x, w
D. w, z, x, y

	Column I		Column II	
13.	w. Joan MacBride	A.	w, x, z, y	13.____
	x. Wm. Mackey	B.	w, y, z, x	
	y. Roslyn McKenzie	C.	w, z, x, y	
	z. Winifred Mackey	D.	w, y , x, z	

	Column I		Column II	
14.	w. 3 Way Trucking Co.	A.	y, x, z, w	14.____
	x. 3rd Street Bakery	B.	y, z, w, x	
	y. 380 Realty Corp.	C.	x, y, z, w	
	z. Three Lions Pub	D.	x, y, w, z	

	Column I		Column II	
15.	w. Miss Rose Leonard	A.	z, w, x, y	15.____
	x. Rev. Leonard Lucas	B.	w, z, y, x	
	y. Sylvia Leonard Linen Shop	C.	w, x, z, y	
	z. Rose S. Leonard	D.	z, w, y, x	

Questions 16-19.

DIRECTIONS: Answer Questions 16 through 19 ONLY on the basis of the information given in the following passage.

Work measurement concerns accomplishment or productivity. It has to do with results; it does not deal with the amount of energy used up, although in many cases this may be in direct proportion to the work output. Work measurement not only helps a manager to distribute work loads fairly, but it also enables him to define work sueeess in actual units, evaluate employee performance, and determine where corrective help is needed. Work measurement is accomplished by measuring the amount produced, measuring the time spent to produce it, and relating the two. To illustrate, it is common to speak of so many orders processed within a given time. The number of orders processed becomes meaningful when related to the amount of time taken.

Much of the work in an office can be measured fairly accurately and inexpensively. The extent of wo.rk measurement possible in any given case will depend upon the particular type of office tasks performed, but usually from two-thirds to three-fourths of all work in an office can be measured. It is true that difficulty in work measurement is encountered, for example, when the office work is irregular and not repeated often, or when the work is primarily mental rather than manual. These are problems, but they are used as excuses for doing no work measurement far more frequently than is justified.

16. According to the above passage, which of the following BEST illustrates the type of information obtained as a result of work measurement? A   16.____

   A. clerk takes one hour to file 150 folders
   B. typist types five letters
   C. stenographer works harder typing from shorthand notes than she does typing from a typed draft
   D. clerk keeps track of employees' time by computing sick leave, annual leave, and overtime leave

17. The above passage does NOT indicate that work measurement can be used to help a supervisor to determine

    A. why an employee is performing poorly on the job
    B. who are the fast and slow workers in the unit
    C. how the work in the unit should be divided up
    D. how long it should take to perform a certain task

18. According to the above passage, the kind of work that would be MOST difficult to measure would be such work as

    A. sorting mail
    B. designing a form for a new procedure
    C. photocopying various materials
    D. answering inquiries with form letters

19. The excuses mentioned in the above passage for failure to perform work measurement can be BEST summarized as the

    A. repetitive nature of office work
    B. costs involved in carrying out accurate work measurement
    C. inability to properly use the results obtained from work measurement
    D. difficulty involved in measuring certain types of work

Questions 20-24.

DIRECTIONS: In each of Questions 20 through 24, there is a sentence containing one under-lined word. Choose the word (lettered A, B, C, or D) which means MOST NEARLY the same as the underlined word as it is used in the sentence.

20. Mr. Warren could not attend the luncheon because he had a prior appointment.

    A. conflicting   B. official
    C. previous   D. important

21. The time allowed to complete the task was not adequate.

    A. long   B. enough   C. excessive   D. required

22. The investigation unit began an extensive search for the information.

    A. complicated   B. superficial
    C. thorough   D. leisurely

23. The secretary answered the telephone in a courteous manner.

    A. businesslike   B. friendly
    C. formal   D. polite

24. The recipient of the money checked the total amount.

    A. receiver   B. carrier   C. borrower   D. giver

25. You receive a telephone call from an employee in another agency requesting information   25.____
about a project being carried out by a division other than your own. You know little about
the work being done, but you would like to help the caller.
Of the following, the BEST action for you to take is to

    A. ask the caller exactly what he would like to know and then tell him all you know
about the work being done
    B. ask the caller to tell you exactly what he would like to know so that you can get the
information while he waits
    C. tell the caller that you will have the call transferred to the division working on the
project
    D. request that the caller write to you so that you can send him the necessary infor-
mation

_____

KEY (CORRECT ANSWERS)

1.	C	11.	D
2.	B	12.	C
3.	C	13.	A
4.	B	14.	C
5.	B	15.	B
6.	C	16.	A
7.	C	17.	A
8.	A	18.	B
9.	D	19.	D
10.	B	20.	C

21.	B
22.	C
23.	D
24.	A
25.	C

_____

TEST 2

DIRECTIONS: Each question or incomplete statement is followed by several suggested answers or completions. Select the one that BEST answers the question or completes the statement. *PRINT THE LETTER OF THE CORRECT ANSWER IN THE SPACE AT THE RIGHT.*

1.   Which of the following actions by a supervisor is LEAST likely to result in an increase in morale or productivity?

   A.   Delegating additional responsibility but not authority to his subordinates
   B.   Spending more time than his subordinates in planning and organizing the office's work
   C.   Giving positive rather than negative orders to his subordinates
   D.   Keeping his subordinates informed about changes in rules or policies which affect their work

Questions 2-8.

DIRECTIONS: Questions 2 through 8 are based SOLELY on the information and the form given below.

The following form is a *Weekly Summary of New Employees* and lists all employees appointed to Department F in the week indicated. In addition to the starting date and name, the form includes each new employee's time card number, title, status, work location and supervisor 's name.

DEPARTMENT F						
Weekly Summary of New Employees					Week Starting March 25	
Start-ing Date	Name Last, First	Time Card No.	Title	Status	Work Location	Supervisor
3/25	Astaire, Hannah	361	Typist	Prov.	Rm. 312	Merrill, Judy
3/25	Silber, Arthur	545	Clerk	Perm.	Rm. 532	Rizzo, Joe
3/26	Vecchio, Robert	620	Accountant	Perm.	Rm. 620	Harper, Ruth
3/26	Goldberg, Sally	373	Stenographer	Prov .	Rm. 308	Merrill, Judy
3/26	Yee, Bruce	555	Accountant	Perm.	Rm. 530	Rizzo, Joe
3/27	Dunning, Betty	469	Typist	Perm.	Rm. 411	Miller, Tony
3/28	Goldman, Sara	576	Stenographer	Prov .	Rm. 532	Rizzo, Joe
3/29	Vesquez, Roy	624	Accountant	Perm.	Rm. 622	Harper, Ruth
3/29	Browning, David	464	Typist	Perm.	Rm. 411	Miller, Tony

2 (#2)

2. On which one of the following dates did two employees *in the same title* begin work?　2.____

    A.　3/25　　　　B.　3/26　　　　C.　3/27　　　　D.　3/29

3. To which one of the following supervisors was ONE typist assigned?　3.____

    A.　Judy Merrill　　　　　　　　B.　Tony Miller
    C.　Ruth Harper　　　　　　　　D.　Joe Rizzo

4. Which one of the following supervisors was assigned the GREATEST number of new　4.____
   employees during the week of March 25?

    A.　Ruth Harper　　　　　　　　B.　Judy Merrill
    C.　Tony Miller　　　　　　　　D.　Joe Rizzo

5. Which one of the following employees was assigned *three days after another employee*　5.____
   to the same job location?

    A.　Sara Goldman　　　　　　　　B.　David Browning
    C.　Bruce Yee　　　　　　　　　　D.　Roy Vesquez

6. The title in which BOTH provisional and permanent appointments were made is　6.____

    A.　accountant　　　B.　clerk　　　C.　stenographer　　D.　typist

7. The employee who started work on the SAME day and have the SAME status but DIF-　7.____
   FERENT titles are

    A.　Arthur Silber and Hannah Astaire
    B.　Robert Vecchio and Bruce Yee
    C.　Sally Goldberg and Sara Goldman
    D.　Roy Vesquez and David Browning

8. On the basis of the information given on the form, which one of the following conclusions　8.____
   regarding time card numbers appears to be CORRECT?

    A.　The first digit of the time card number is coded according to the assigned title.
    B.　The middle digit of the time card number is coded according to the assigned title.
    C.　The first digit of the time card number is coded according to the employees' floor
       locations.
    D.　Time card numbers are randomly assigned.

9. Assume that a caller arrives at your desk and states that she is your supervisor's daugh-　9.____
   ter and that she would like to see her father. You have been under the impression that
   your supervisor has only a two-year-old son.
   Of the following, the BEST way to deal with this visitor is to

    A.　offer her a seat and advise your supervisor of the visitor
    B.　tell her to go right in to her father's office
    C.　ask her for some proof to show that she is your supervisor's daughter
    D.　escort her into your supervisor's office and ask him if the visitor is his daughter

10. Assume that you answer the telephone and the caller says that he is a police officer and　10.____
    asks for personal information about one of your co-workers.
    Of the following, the BEST course of action for you to take is to

A.   give the caller the information he has requested
B.   ask the caller for the telephone number of the phone he is using, call him back, and then give him the information
C.   refuse to give him any information and offer to transfer the call to your supervisor
D.   ask the caller for his name and badge number before giving him the information

Questions 11-16.

DIRECTIONS: Questions 11 through 16 each consist of a sentence which may or may not be an example of good English usage. Consider grammar, punctuation, spelling, capitalization, awkwardness, etc. Examine each sentence, and then choose the correct statement about it from the four choices below it. If the English usage in the sentence given is better than it would be with any of the changes suggested in Options B, C, or D, choose Option A. Do not choose an option that will change the meaning of the sentence.

11.   The recruiting officer said, *"There are many different goverment jobs available."*   11.

  A.   This is an example of acceptable writing.
  B.   The word *There* should not be capitalized.
  C.   The word *goverment* should be spelled *government.*
  D.   The comma after the word *said* should be removed.

12.   He can recommend a mechanic whose work is reliable.   12.

  A.   This is an example of acceptable writing.
  B.   The word *reliable* should be spelled *relyable.*
  C.   The word *whose* should be spelled *who's.*
  D.   The word *mechanic* should be spelled *mecanic.*

13.   She typed quickly; like someone who had not a moment to lose.   13

  A.   This is an example of acceptable writing.
  B.   The word *not* should be removed.
  C.   The semicolon should be changed to a comma.
  D.   The word *quickly* should be placed before instead of after the word *typed.*

14.   She insisted that she had to much work to do.   14

  A.   This is an example of acceptable writing.
  B.   The word *insisted* should be spelled *incisted.*
  C.   The word *to* used in front of *much* should be spelled *too.*
  D.   The word *do* should be changed to *be done.*

15.   He excepted praise from his supervisor for a job well done.   15

  A.   This is an example of acceptable writing.
  B.   The word *excepted* should be spelled *accepted.*
  C.   The order of the words *well done* should be changed to *done well.*
  D.   There should be a comma after the word,*supervisor*

16. What appears to be intentional errors in grammar occur several times in the passage.   16._____

    A. This is an example of acceptable writing.
    B. The word *occur* should be spelled *occurr.*
    C. The word *appears* should be changed to *appear.*
    D. The phrase *several times* should be changed to *from time to time.*

17. The daily compensation to be paid to each consultant hired in a certain agency is com-   17._____
puted by dividing his professional earnings in the previous year by 250. The maximum
daily compensation they can receive is $200 each. Four consultants who were hired to
work on a special project had the following professional earnings in the previous year:
$37,500, $44,000, $46,500, and $61,100.
What will be the TOTAL DAILY COST to the agency for these four consultants?

    A. $932   B. $824   C. $756   D. $712

18. In a typing and stenographic pool consisting of 30 employees, 2/5 of them are typists,   18._____
1/3 of them are senior typists and senior stenographers, and the rest are stenographers.
If there are 5 more stenographers than senior stenographers, how many senior stenographers are in the typing and stenographic pool?

    A. 3   B. 5   C. 8   D. 10

19. There are 3330 copies of a three-page report to be collated. One clerk starts collating at   19._____
9:00 A.M. and is joined 15 minutes later by two other clerks. It takes 15 minutes for each
of these clerks to collate 90 copies of the report.
At what time should the job be completed if ALL three clerks continue working at the
SAME rate without breaks?

    A. 12:00 Noon   B. 12:15 P.M.   C. 1:00 P.M.   D. 1:15 P.M.

20. By the end of last year, membership in the blood credit program in a certain agency had   20._____
increased from the year before by 500, bringing the total to 2500.
If the membership increased by the same percentage this year, the TOTAL number of
members in the blood credit program for this agency by the end of this year should be

    A. 2625   B. 3000   C. 3125   D. 3250

21. During this year, an agency suggestion program put into practice suggestions from 24   21._____
employees, thereby saving the agency 40 times the amount of money it paid in awards.
If 1/3 of the employees were awarded $50 each, 1/2 of the employees were awarded
$25 each, and the rest were awarded $10 each, how much money did the agency
SAVE by using the suggestions?

    A. $18,760   B. $29,600   C. $32,400   D. $46,740

22. Which of the following actions should a supervisor generally find MOST effective as a   22._____
method of determining whether subordinates need additional training in performing their
work?

    A. Compiling a list of absences and latenesses of subordinates
    B. Observing the manner in which his subordinates carry out their various tasks
    C. Reviewing the grievances submitted by subordinates
    D. Reminding his subordinates to consult him if they experience difficulty in complet-
ing an assignment

23. Of the following types of letters, the MOST difficult to trace if lost after mailing is the _____ letter.

    A. special delivery   B. registered
    C. insured   D. certified

24. Suppose that you are looking over a few incoming letters that have been put in your mail basket. You see that one has a return address on the envelope but not on the letter itself. Of the following, the BEST way to make sure there is a correct record of the return address is to

    A. return the letter to the sender and ask him to fill in his address on his own letter
    B. put the letter back into the envelope and close the opening with a paper clip
    C. copy the address onto a 3"x5" index card and throw away the envelope
    D. copy the address onto the letter and staple the envelope to the letter

25. Although most incoming mail that you receive in an office will pertain to business matters, there are times when a letter may be delivered for your supervisor that is marked *Personal*.
    Of the following, the BEST way for you to handle this type of mail is to

    A. open the letter but do not read it, and route it along with the other mail
    B. read the letter to see if it really is personal
    C. have the letter forwarded unopened to your supervisor's home address
    D. deliver the letter to your supervisor's desk unopened

KEY (CORRECT ANSWERS)

1. A		11. C	
2. B		12. A	
3. A		13. C	
4. D		14. C	
5. A		15. B	
6. D		16. C	
7. D		17. D	
8. C		18. A	
9. A		19. B	
10. C		20. C	

21. B
22. B
23. D
24. D
25. D

READING COMPREHENSION
UNDERSTANDING AND INTERPRETING WRITTEN MATERIAL
EXAMINATION SECTION
TEST 1

DIRECTIONS: Each question or incomplete statement is followed by several suggested
answers or completions. Select the one that BEST answers the question or
completes the statement. *PRINT THE LETTER OF THE CORRECT ANSWER
IN THE SPACE AT THE RIGHT.*

Questions 1-4.

DIRECTIONS: Questions 1 through 4 are to be answered SOLELY on the basis of the following passage.

Those engaged in the exercise of First Amendment rights by pickets, marches, parades,
and open-air assemblies are not exempted from obeying valid local traffic ordinances. In a
recent pronouncement, Mr. Justice Baxter, speaking for the Supreme Court, wrote:

The rights of free speech and assembly, while fundamental to our democratic society, still
do not mean that everyone with opinions or beliefs to express may address a group at any
public place and at any time. The constitutional guarantee of liberty implies the existence of
an organized society maintaining public order, without which liberty itself would be lost in the
excesses of anarchy. The control of travel on the streets is a clear example of governmental
responsibility to insure this necessary order. A restriction in that relation, designed to promote
the public convenience in the interest of all, and not susceptible to abuses of discriminatory
application, cannot be disregarded by the attempted exercise of some civil rights which, in
other circumstances, would be entitled to protection. One would not be justified in ignoring
the familiar red light because this was thought to be a means of social protest. Governmental
authorities have the duty and responsibility to keep their streets open and available for move-
ment. A group of demonstrators could not insist upon the right to cordon off a street, or
entrance to a public or private building, and allow no one to pass who did not agree to listen
to their exhortations.

1.   Which of the following statements BEST reflects Mr. Justice Baxter's view of the relation-   1._____
ship between liberty and public order?

    A.   Public order cannot exist without liberty.
    B.   Liberty cannot exist without public order.
    C.   The existence of liberty undermines the existence of public order.
    D.   The maintenance of public order insures the existence of liberty.

2.   According to the above passage, local traffic ordinances result from   2._____

    A.   governmental limitations on individual liberty
    B.   governmental responsibility to insure public order
    C.   majority rule as determined by democratic procedures
    D.   restrictions on expression of dissent

3. The above passage suggests that government would be acting improperly if a local traffic ordinance

     A. was enforced in a discriminatory manner
     B. resulted in public inconvenience
     C. violated the right of free speech and assembly
     D. was not essential to public order

4. Of the following, the MOST appropriate title for the above passage is

     A. THE RIGHTS OF FREE SPEECH AND ASSEMBLY
     B. ENFORCEMENT OF LOCAL TRAFFIC ORDINANCES
     C. FIRST AMENDMENT RIGHTS AND LOCAL TRAFFIC ORDINANCES
     D. LIBERTY AND ANARCHY

Questions 5-8

DIRECTIONS: Questions 5 through 8 are to be answered SOLELY on the basis of the following passage

On November 8, 1976, the Supreme Court refused to block the payment of Medicaid funds for elective abortions. The Court's action means that a new Federal statute that bars the use of Federal funds for abortions unless abortion is necessary to save the life of the mother will not go into effect for many months, if at all.

A Federal District Court in Brooklyn ruled the following month that the statute was unconstitutional and ordered that Federal reimbursement for the costs of abortions continue on the same basis as reimbursements for the costs of pregnancy and childbirth-related services.

Technically, what the Court did today was to deny a request by Senator Howard Ramsdell and others for a stay blocking enforcement of the District Court order pending appeal. The Court's action was a victory for New York City. The City's Health and Hospitals Corporation initiated one of the two lawsuits challenging the new statute that led to the District Court's decision. The Corporation also opposed the request for a Supreme Court stay of that decision, telling the Court in a memorandum that a stay would subject the Corporation to a *grave and irreparable injury.*

5. According to the above passage, it would be CORRECT to state that the Health and Hospitals Corporation

     A. joined Senator Ramsdell in his request for a stay
     B. opposed the statute which limited reimbursement for the cost of abortions
     C. claimed that it would experience a loss if the District Court order was enforced
     D. appealed the District Court decision

6. The above passage indicates that the Supreme Court acted in DIRECT response to

     A. a lawsuit initiated by the Health and Hospitals Corporation
     B. a ruling by a Federal District Court
     C. a request for a stay
     D. the passage of a new Federal statute

7. According to the above passage, it would be CORRECT to state that the Supreme Court   7.____

    A. blocked enforcement of the District Court order
    B. refused a request for a stay to block enforcement of the Federal statute
    C. ruled that the new Federal statute was unconstitutional
    D. permitted payment of Federal funds for abortion to continue

8. Following are three statements concerning abortion that might be correct: 8.____
    I. Abortion costs are no longer to be Federally reimbursed on the same basis as those for pregnancy and childbirth
    II. Federal funds have not been available for abortions except to save the life of the mother
    III. Medicaid has paid for elective abortions in the past
According to the passage above, which of the following CORRECTLY classifies the above statements into those that are true and those that are not true?

    A. I is true, but II and III are not.
    B. I and III are true, but II is not.
    C. I and II are true, but III is not.
    D. III is true, but I and II are not.

Questions 9-12.

DIRECTIONS: Questions 9 through 12 are to be answered SOLELY on the basis of the following passage.

    A person may use physical force upon another person when and to the extent he reasonably believes such to be necessary to defend himself or a third person from what he reasonably believes to be the use or imminent use of unlawful physical force by such other person, unless (a) the latter's conduct was provoked by the actor himself with intent to cause physical injury to another person; or (b) the actor was the initial aggressor; or (c) the physical force involved is the product of a combat by agreement not specifically authorized by law.

    A person may not use deadly physical force upon another person under the circumstances specified above unless (a) he reasonably believes that such other person is using or is about to use deadly physical force. Even in such case, however, the actor may not use deadly physical force if he knows he can, with complete safety, as to himself and others avoid the necessity of doing so by retreating; except that he is under no duty to retreat if he is in his dwelling and is not the initial aggressor; or (b) he reasonably believes that such other person is committing or attempting to commit a kidnapping, forcible rape, or forcible sodomy.

9. Jones and Smith, who have not met before, get into an argument in a tavern. Smith takes   9.____
a punch at Jones, but misses. Jones then hits Smith on the chin with his fist. Smith falls to the floor and suffers minor injuries.
According to the above passage, it would be CORRECT to state that _____ justified in using physical force.

    A. only Smith was   B. only Jones was
    C. both Smith and Jones were   D. neither Smith nor Jones was

10. While walking down the street, Brady observes Miller striking Mrs. Adams on the head with his fist in an attempt to steal her purse.
According to the above passage, it would be CORRECT to state that Brady would

   A. not be justified in using deadly physical force against Miller since Brady can safely retreat
   B. be justified in using physical force against Miller but not deadly physical force
   C. not be justified in using physical force against Miller since Brady himself is not being attacked
   D. be justified in using deadly physical force

11. Winters is attacked from behind by Sharp, who attempts to beat up Winters with a black-jack. Winters disarms Sharp and succeeds in subduing him with a series of blows to the head. Sharp stops fighting and explains that he thought Winters was the person who had robbed his apartment a few minutes before, but now realizes his mistake.
According to the above passage, it would be CORRECT to state that

   A. Winters was justified in using physical force on Sharp only to the extent necessary to defend himself
   B. Winters was not justified in using physical force on Sharp since Sharp's attack was provoked by what he believed to be Winters' behavior
   C. Sharp was justified in using physical force on Winters since he reasonably believed that Winters had unlawfully robbed him
   D. Winters was justified in using physical force on Sharp only because Sharp was acting mistakenly in attacking him

12. Roberts hears a noise in the cellar of his home, and, upon investigation, discovers an intruder, Welch. Welch moves towards Roberts in a threatening manner, thrusts his hand into a bulging pocket, and withdraws what appears to be a gun. Roberts thereupon strikes Welch over the head with a golf club. He then sees that the *gun* is a toy. Welch later dies of head injuries. According to the above passage, it would be CORRECT to state that Roberts was

   A. justified in using deadly physical force because he reasonably believed Welch was about to use deadly physical force
   B. not justified in using deadly physical force
   C. justified in using deadly physical force only because he did not provoke Welch's conduct
   D. justified in using deadly physical force only because he was not the initial aggressor

Questions 13-16.

DIRECTIONS: Questions 13 through 16 are to be answered SOLELY on the basis of the following passage.

From the beginning, the Supreme Court has supervised the fairness of trials conducted by the Federal government. But the Constitution, as originally drafted, gave the court no such general authority in state cases. The court's power to deal with state cases comes from the Fourteenth Amendment, which became part of the Constitution in 1868. The crucial provision forbids any state to *deprive any person of life, liberty, or property without due process of law.*

The guarantee of *due process* would seem, at the least, to require fair procedure in criminal trials. But curiously the Supreme Court did not speak on the question for many decades. During that time, however, the due process clause was interpreted to bar *unreasonable* state economic regulations, such as minimum wage laws.

In 1915, there came the case of Leo M. Frank, a Georgian convicted of murder in a trial that he contended was dominated by mob hysteria. Historians now agree that there was such hysteria, with overtones of anti-semitism.

The Supreme Court held that it could not look past the findings of the Georgia courts that there had been no mob atmosphere at the trial. Justices Oliver Wendell Holmes and Charles Evans Hughes dissented, arguing that the constitutional guarantee would be *a barren one* if the Federal courts could not make their own inferences from the facts.

In 1923, the case of Moore v. Dempsey involved five Arkansas Blacks convicted of murder and sentenced to death in a community so aroused against them that at one point they were saved from lynching only by Federal troops. Witnesses against them were said to have been beaten into testifying.

The court, though not actually setting aside the convictions, directed a lower Federal court to hold a habeas corpus hearing to find out whether the trial had been fair, or whether the whole proceeding had been *a mask—that counsel, jury, and judge were swept to the fatal end by an irresistible wave of public passion.*

13. According to the above passage, the Supreme Court's INITIAL interpretation of the Fourteenth Amendment   13.____

    A. protected state supremacy in economic matters
    B. increased the scope of Federal jurisdiction
    C. required fair procedures in criminal trials
    D. prohibited the enactment of minimum wage laws

14. According to the above passage, the Supreme Court in the Frank case   14.____

    A. denied that there had been mob hysteria at the trial
    B. decided that the guilty verdict was supported by the evidence
    C. declined to question the state court's determination of the facts
    D. found that Leo Frank had not received *due process*

15. According to the above passage, the dissenting judges in the Frank case maintained that   15.____

    A. due process was an empty promise in the circumstances of that case
    B. the Federal courts could not guarantee certain provisions of the Constitution
    C. the Federal courts should not make their own inferences from the facts in state cases
    D. the Supreme Court had rendered the Constitution *barren*

16. Of the following, the MOST appropriate title for the above passage is

    A. THE CONDUCT OF FEDERAL TRIALS
    B. THE DEVELOPMENT OF STATES' RIGHTS: 1868-1923
    C. MOORE V. DEMPSEY: A CASE STUDY IN CRIMINAL JUSTICE
    D. DUE PROCESS-THE EVOLUTION OF A CONSTITUTIONAL CORNERSTONE

Questions 17-20.

DIRECTIONS: Questions 17 through 20 are to be answered SOLELY on the basis of the following passage.

The difficulty experienced in determining which party has the burden of proving payment or non-payment is due largely to a lack of consistency between the rules of pleading and the rules of proof. In some cases, a plaintiff is obligated by a rule of pleading to allege non-payment on his complaint, yet is not obligated to prove non-payment on the trial. An action upon a contract for the payment of money will serve as an illustration. In such a case, the plaintiff must allege non-payment in his complaint, but the burden of proving payment on the trial is upon the defendant. An important and frequently cited case on this problem is Conkling v. Weatherwax. In that case, the action was brought to establish and enforce a legacy as a lien upon real property. The defendant alleged in her answer that the legacy had been paid. There was no witness competent to testify for the plaintiff to show that the legacy had not been paid. Therefore, the question of the burden of proof became of primary importance since, if the plaintiff had the burden of proving non-payment, she must fail in her action; whereas if the burden of proof was on the defendant to prove payment, the plaintiff might win. The Court of Appeals held that the burden of proof was on the plaintiff. In the course of his opinion, Judge Vann attempted to harmonize the conflicting cases on this subject, and for that purpose formulated three rules. These rules have been construed and applied to numerous subsequent cases. As so construed and applied, these may be summarized as follows:

Rule 1.   In an action upon a contract for the payment of money only, where the complaint does not allege a balance due over and above all payments made, the plaintiff must allege nonpayment in his complaint, but the burden of proving payment is upon the defendant. In such a case, payment is an affirmative defense which the defendant must plead in his answer. If the defendant fails to plead payment, but pleads a general denial instead, he will not be permitted to introduce evidence of payment.

Rule 2.   Where the complaint sets forth a balance in excess of all payments, owing to the structure of the pleading, burden is upon the plaintiff to prove his allegation. In this case, the defendant is not required to plead payment as a defense in his answer but may introduce evidence of payment under a general denial.

Rule 3.   When the action is not upon contract for the payment of money, but is upon an obligation created by operation of law, or is for the enforcement of a lien where non-payment of the amount secured is part of the cause of action, it is necessary both to allege and prove the fact of nonpayment.

17. In the above passage, the case of Conkling v. Weatherwax was cited PRIMARILY to illustrate   17.____

    A. a case where the burden of proof was on the defendant to prove payment
    B. how the question of the burden of proof can affect the outcome of a case
    C. the effect of a legacy as a lien upon real property
    D. how conflicting cases concerning the burden of proof were harmonized

18. According to the above passage, the pleading of payment is a defense in Rule(s)   18.____

    A. 1, but not Rules 2 and 3
    B. 2, but not Rules 1 and 3
    C. 1 and 3, but not Rule 2
    D. 2 and 3, but not Rule 1

19. The facts in Conkling v. Weatherwax CLOSELY resemble the conditions described in   19.____

    A. Rule #1
    B. Rule #2
    C. Rule #3
    D. none of the rules

20. The MAJOR topic of the above passage may BEST be described as   20.____

    A. determining the ownership of property
    B. providing a legal definition
    C. placing the burden of proof
    D. formulating rules for deciding cases

Questions 21-25.

DIRECTIONS: Questions 21 through 25 are to be answered SOLELY on the basis of the following passage.

    The law is quite clear that evidence obtained in violation of Section 605 of the Federal Communications Act is not admissible in Federal court. However, the law as to the admissibility of evidence in state court is far from clear. Had the Supreme Court of the United States made the wiretap exclusionary rule applicable to the states, such confusion would not exist.

    In the case of Alton v. Texas, the Supreme Court was called upon to determine whether wiretapping by state and local officers came within the proscription of the Federal statute and, if so, whether Section 605 required the same remedies for its vindication in state courts. In answer to the first question, Mr. Justice Minton, speaking for the court, flatly stated that Section 605 made it a federal crime for anyone to intercept telephone messages and divulge what he learned. The court went on to say that a state officer who testified in state court concerning the existence, contents, substance, purport, effect, or meaning of an intercepted conversation violated the Federal law and committed a criminal act. In regard to the second question, how-ever, the Supreme Court felt constrained by due regard for federal-state relations to answer in the negative. Mr. Justice Minton stated that the court would not presume, in the absence of a clear manifestation of congressional intent, that Congress intended to supersede state rules of evidence.

Because the Supreme Court refused to apply the exclusionary rule to wiretap evidence that was being used in state courts, the states respectively made this decision for themselves. According to hearings held before a congressional committee in 1975, six states authorize wiretapping by statute, 33 states impose total bans on wiretapping, and 11 states have no definite statute on the subject. For examples of extremes, a statute in Pennsylvania will be compared with a statute in New York.

The Pennsylvania statute provides that no communications by telephone or telegraph can be intercepted without permission of both parties. It also specifically prohibits such interception by public officials and provides that evidence obtained cannot be used in court.

The lawmakers in New York, recognizing the need for legal wire-tapping, authorized wiretapping by statute. A New York law authorizes the issuance of an ex parte order upon oath or affirmation for limited wiretapping. The aim of the New York law is to allow court-ordered wiretapping and to encourage the testimony of state officers concerning such wiretapping in court. The New York law was found to be constitutional by the New York State Supreme Court in 1975. Other states, including Oregon, Maryland, Nevada, and Massachusetts, enacted similar laws which authorize court-ordered wiretapping.

To add to this legal disarray, the vast majority of the states, including New Jersey and New York, permit wiretapping evidence to be received in court even though obtained in violation of the state laws and of Section 605 of the Federal act. However, some states, such as Rhode Island, have enacted statutory exclusionary rules which provide that illegally procured wiretap evidence is incompetent in civil as well as criminal actions.

21. According to the above passage, a state officer who testifies in New York State court concerning the contents of a conversation he overheard through a court-ordered wire-tap is in violation of _____ law.

    A. state law but not federal
    B. federal law but not state
    C. federal law and state
    D. neither federal nor state

22. According to the above passage, which of the following statements concerning states statutes on wiretapping is CORRECT?

    A. The number of states that impose total bans on wiretapping is three times as great as the number of states with no definite statute on wiretapping.
    B. The number of states having no definite statute on wiretapping is more than twice the number of states authorizing wiretapping.
    C. The number of states which authorize wiretapping by statute and the number of states having no definite statute on wiretapping exceed the number of states imposing total bans on wiretapping.
    D. More states authorize wiretapping by statute than impose total bans on wiretapping.

23. Following are three statements concerning wiretapping that might be valid: 23.____
    I.   In Pennsylvania, only public officials may legally intercept telephone commu-
         nications.
    II. In Rhode Island, evidence obtained through an illegal wiretap is incompetent
         in criminal, but not civil, actions.
    III. Neither Massachusetts nor Pennsylvania authorizes wiretapping by public
         officials.

    According to the above passage, which of the following CORRECTLY classifies these
    statements into those that are valid and those that are not?

    A.   I is valid, but II and III are not.
    B.   II is valid, but I and III are not.
    C.   II and III are valid, but I is not.
    D.   None of the statements is valid.

24. According to the above passage, evidence obtained in violation of Section 605 of the   24.____
    Federal Communications Act is inadmissible in

    A.   federal court but not in any state courts
    B.   federal court and all state courts
    C.   all state courts but not in federal court
    D.   federal court and some state courts

25. In regard to state rules of evidence, Mr. Justice Minton expressed the Court's opinion   25.____
    that Congress

    A.   intended to supersede state rules of evidence, as manifested by Section 605 of the
         Federal Communications Act
    B.   assumed that federal statutes would govern state rules of evidence in all wiretap
         cases
    C.   left unclear whether it intended to supersede state rules of evidence
    D.   precluded itself from superseding state rules of evidence through its regard for fed-
         eral-state relations

KEY (CORRECT ANSWERS)

1.	B		11.	A
2.	B		12.	A
3.	A		13.	D
4.	C		14.	C
5.	B		15.	A
6.	C		16.	D
7.	D		17.	B
8.	D		18.	A
9.	B		19.	C
10.	B		20.	C

21.	B
22.	A
23.	D
24.	D
25.	C

TEST 2

DIRECTIONS: Each question or incomplete statement is followed by several suggested answers or completions. Select the one that BEST answers the question or completes the Statement. *PRINT THE LETTER OF THE CORRECT ANSWER IN THE SPACE AT THE RIGHT.*

Questions 1-3.

DIRECTIONS: Questions 1 through 3 are to be answered SOLELY on the basis of the following passage.

The State Assembly has passed a bill that would require all state agencies, public authorities, and local governments to refuse bids in excess of $2,000 from any foreign firm or corporation. The only exceptions to this outright prohibition against public buying of foreign goods or services would be for products not available in this country, goods of a quality unobtainable from an American supplier, and products using foreign materials that are *substantially* manufactured in the United States.

This bill is a flagrant violation of the United States' officially espoused trade principles. It would add to the costs of state and local governments. It could provoke retaliatory action from many foreign governments against the state and other American producers, and foreign governments would be fully entitled to take such retaliatory action under the General Agreement on Tariffs and Trade, which the United States has signed.

The State Senate, which now has the Assembly bill before it, should reject this protectionist legislation out of enlightened regard for the interests of the taxpayers and producers of the State—as well as for those of the nation and its trading partners generally. In this time of unemployment and international monetary disorder, the State—with its reputation for intelligent and progressive law-making—should avoid contributing to what could become a tidal wave of protectionism here and overseas.

1. Under the requirements of the bill passed by the State Assembly, a bid from a foreign manufacturer in excess of $2,000 can be accepted by a state agency or local government only if it meets which one of the following requirements?
   The

    A. bid is approved individually by the State Legislature
    B. bidder is willing to accept payment in United States currency
    C. bid is for an item of a quality unobtainable from an American supplier
    D. bid is for an item which would be more expensive if it were purchased from an American supplier

1.____

2. The author of the above passage feels that the bill passed by the State Assembly should be

    A. passed by the State Senate and put into effect
    B. passed by the State Senate but vetoed by the Governor
    C. reintroduced into the State Assembly and rejected
    D. rejected by the State Senate

2.____

3. The author of the above passage calls the practice of prohibiting purchase of products manufactured by foreign countries

    A. prohibition   B. protectionism
    C. retaliatory action   D. isolationism

Questions 4-7.

DIRECTIONS: Questions 4 through 7 are to be answered SOLELY on the basis of the following passage.

Data processing is by no means a new invention. In one form or another, it has been carried on throughout the entire history of civilization. In its most general sense, data processing means organizing data so that it can be used for a specific purpose-a procedure commonly known simply as *record-keeping* or *paperwork*. With the development of modern office equipment, and particularly with the recent introduction of computers, the techniques of data processing have become highly elaborate and sophisticated, but the basic purpose remains the same: Turning raw data into useful information.

The key concept here is usefulness. The data, or input, that is to be processed can be compared to the raw material that is to go into a manufacturing process. The information, or output, that results from data processing—like the finished product of a manufacturer—should be clearly usable. A collection of data has little value unless it is converted into information that serves a specific function.

4. The expression *paperwork,* as it is used in this passage,

    A. shows that the author regards such operations as a waste of time
    B. has the same general meaning as *data processing*
    C. refers to methods of record-keeping that are no longer in use
    D. indicates that the public does not understand the purpose of data processing

5. The above passage indicates that the use of computers has

    A. greatly simplified the clerical work in an office
    B. led to more complicated systems for the handling of data
    C. had no effect whatsoever on data processing
    D. made other modern office machines obsolete

6. Which of the following BEST expresses the basic principle of data processing as it is described in the above passage?

    A. Input-processing-output
    B. Historical record-keeping-modern techniques -specific functions
    C. Office equipment-computer-accurate data
    D. Raw material-manufacturer-retailer

7. According to the above passage, data processing may be described as

    A. a new management technique
    B. computer technology
    C. information output
    D. record-keeping

Questions 8-10.

DIRECTIONS: Questions 8 through 10 are to be answered SOLELY on the basis of the following passage.

A loan receipt is an instrument devised to permit the insurance company to bring an
action against the wrongdoer in the name of the insured despite the fact that the insured no
longer has any financial interest in the outcome. It provides, in effect, that the amount of the
loss is advanced to the insured as a loan which is repayable only up to the extent of any
recovery made from the wrongdoer. The insured further agrees to enter and prosecute suit
against the wrongdoer in his own name. Such a receipt substitutes a loan for a payment for
the purpose of permitting the insurance company to press its action against the wrongdoer in
the name of the insured.

8. According to the above passage, the purpose behind the use of a loan receipt is to   8.____

   A. guarantee that the insurance company gets repayment from the person insured
   B. insure repayment of all expenditures to the named insured
   C. make it possible for the insurance company to sue in the name of the policyowner
   D. prevent the wrongdoer from escaping the natural consequences of his act

9. According to the above passage, the amount of the loan which must be paid back to the   9.____
   insurance company equals but does NOT exceed the amount

   A. of the loss
   B. on the face of the policy
   C. paid to the insured
   D. recovered from the wrongdoer

10. According to the above passage, by giving a loan receipt, the person insured agrees to   10.____

   A. a suit against the wrongdoer in his own name
   B. forego any financial gain from the outcome of the suit
   C. institute an action on behalf of the insurance company
   D. repay the insurance company for the loan received

Questions 11-12.

DIRECTIONS: Questions 11 and 12 are to be answered SOLELY on the basis of the following
passage.

Open air markets originally came into existence spontaneously when groups of pushcart
peddlers congregated in spots where business was good. Good business induced them to
return to these spots daily and, thus, unofficial open air markets arose. These peddlers paid
no fees, and the city received no revenue from them. Confusion and disorder reigned in these
unsupervised markets; the earliest arrivals secured the best locations, unless or until forcibly
ejected by stronger or tougher peddlers. Although the open air markets supplied a definite
need in the community, there were many detrimental factors involved in their operation. They
were unsightly, created unsanitary conditions in market streets by the deposit of garbage and
waste and were a definite obstruction to traffic, as well as a fire hazard.

11. On the basis of the above passage, the MOST accurate of the following statements is:

    A. Each peddler in the original open air markets had his own fixed location.
    B. Open air markets were originally organized by means of agreements between groups of pushcart peddlers.
    C. The locations of these markets depended upon the amount of business the vendors were able to do.
    D. There was confusion and disorder in these open air markets because the peddlers were not required to pay any fees to the city.

12. Of the following, the MOST valid implication which can be made on the basis of the above passage is that the

    A. detrimental aspect of the operations of open air markets was the probable reason for the creation of enclosed markets under the supervision of the Department of Markets
    B. open air markets could not supply any community need without proper supervision
    C. original open air markets were good examples of the operation of fair competition in business
    D. possibility of obtaining a source of revenue was probably the most important reason for the city's ultimate undertaking of the supervision of open air markets

Questions 13-14.

DIRECTIONS: Questions 13 and 14 are to be answered SOLELY on the basis of the following passage.

A person who displays on his window, door, or in his place of business words or letters in Hebraic characters other than the word *kosher,* or any sign, emblem, insignia, six-pointed star, symbol or mark in simulation of same, without displaying in conjunction there-with in English letters of at least the same size as such characters, signs, emblems, insignia or marks, the words *we sell kosher meat and food only* or *we sell non-kosher meat and food only* or *we sell both kosher and non-kosher meat and food,* as the case may be, is guilty of a misdemeanor. Possession of non-kosher meat and food in any place of business advertising the sale of kosher meat and food only is presumptive evidence that the person in possession exposes the same for sale with intent to defraud, in violation of the provisions of this section.

13. Of the following, the MOST valid implication that can be made on the basis of the above passage is that a person who

    A. displays on his window a six-pointed star in addition to the word *kosher* in Hebraic letters is guilty of intent to defraud
    B. displays on his window the word *kosher* in Hebraic characters intends to indicate that he has only kosher food for sale
    C. sells both kosher and non-kosher food in the same place of business is guilty of a misdemeanor
    D. sells only that type of food which can be characterized as neither kosher nor non-kosher, such as fruit and vegetables, without an explanatory sign in English is guilty of intent to defraud

14. Of the following, the one which would constitute a violation of the rules of the above pas- 14.____
    sage is a case in which a person
    A. displays the word *kosher* on his window in Hebraic letters has only kosher meat
       and food in the store but has some non-kosher meat in the rear of the establish-
       ment
    B. selling both kosher and non-kosher meat and food uses words in Hebraic letters,
       other than the word *kosher,* on his window and a sign of the same size letters in
       English stating *we sell both kosher and non-kosher meat and food*
    C. selling only kosher meat and food uses words in Hebraic letters, other than the
       word *kosher,* on his window and a sign of the same size letters in English stating
       we sell kosher meat and food only
    D. selling only non-kosher meat and food displays a six-pointed star on his window
       and a sign of the same size letters in English stating *we sell only non-kosher meat
       and food*

Questions 15-16.

DIRECTIONS: Questions 15 and 16 are to be answered SOLELY on the basis of the following
              passage.

COMMODITIES IN GLASS BOTTLES OR JARS

The contents of the bottle may be stated in terms of weight or of fluid measure, the
weight being indicated in terms of pounds and ounces and the fluid measure being indicated
in terms of gallons, quarts, pints, half-pints, gills, or fluid ounces. When contents are liquid,
the amount should not be stated in terms of weight. The marking indicating content is to be
on a tag attached to the bottle or upon a label. The letters shall be in bold-faced type at least
one-ninth of an inch (1/9") in height for bottles or jars having a capacity of a gill, half-pint, pint,
or multiples of a pint, and letters at least three-sixteenths of an inch (3/16") in height for bottles of other capacities, on a part of the tag or label free from other printing or ornamentation,
leaving a clear space around the marking which indicates the contents.

15. Of the following, the one which does NOT meet the requirements of the above passage 15.____
    is a
    A. bottle of cooking oil with a label stating *contents—16 fluid ounces* in appropriate
       sized letters
    B. bottle of vinegar with a label stating *contents—8 ounces avoir.* in appropriate sized
       letters
    C. glass jar filled with instant coffee with a label stating *contents—1 lb. 3 ozs. avoir.* in
       appropriate sized letters
    D. glass jar filled with liquid bleach with a label stating *contents—1 quart* in appropriate
       sized letters

16. Of the following, the one which does meet the requirements of the above passage is a 16.____
    A. bottle filled with a low-calorie liquid sweetener with a label stating *contents—3 fluid
       ounces* in letters 1/12" high
    B. bottle filled with ammonia solution for cleaning with a label stating *contents—1 pint* in
       letters 1/10" high

C. jar filled with baking powder with a label stating *contents*—$\frac{1}{2}$ *pint* in letters $\frac{1}{4}$" high

D. jar filled with hard candy with a label stating *contents*—*1 lb. avoir.* in letters $\frac{1}{2}$" high

Question 17.

DIRECTIONS: Question 17 is to be answered SOLELY on the basis of the information contained in the following passage.

DEALERS IN SECOND HAND DEVICES

1. It shall be unlawful for any person to engage in or conduct the business of dealing in, trading in, selling, receiving, or repairing condemned, rebuilt, or used weighing or measuring devices without a permit therefor.

2. Such permit shall expire on the twenty-eighth day of February next succeeding the date of issuance thereof.

3. Every person engaged in the above business, within five days after the making of a repair, or the sale and delivery of a repaired, rebuilt, or used weighing or measuring device, shall serve notice in writing on the commissioner giving the name and address of the person for whom the repair has been made or to whom a repaired, rebuilt, or used weighing or measuring device has been sold or delivered, and shall include a statement that such device has been so altered, repaired, or rebuilt as to conform to the regulations of the department.

17. According to the above passage, the MOST accurate of the following statements is:

A. A permit issued to engage in the business mentioned above, first issued on April 23, 1968, expired on February 28, 1969.
B. A rebuilt or repaired weighing or measuring device should not operate with less error than the tolerances permitted by the regulations of the department.
C. If a used scale in good condition is sold, it is not necessary for the seller to notify the commissioner of the name and address of the buyer.
D. There is a difference in the time required to notify the commissioner of a repair or of a sale of a repaired device.

Questions 18-19.

DIRECTIONS: Questions 18 and 19 are to be answered SOLELY on the basis of the following passage.

A. It shall be unlawful for any person, firm, or corporation to sell or offer for sale at retail for use in internal combustion engines in motor vehicles any gasoline unless such seller shall post and keep continuously posted on the individual pump or other dispensing device from which such gasoline is sold or offered for sale a sign or placard not less than seven inches in height and eight inches in width nor larger than twelve inches in height and twelve inches in width and stating clearly in numbers of uniform size the selling price or prices per gallon of such gasoline so sold or offered for sale from such pump or other dispensing device.

B.   The amount of governmental tax to be collected in connection with the sale of such gasoline shall be stated on such sign or placard and separately and apart from such selling price or prices.

18.   The one of the following price signs posted on a gasoline pump which would be in viola-   18.____
tion of the above passage is a sign _____ square inches in size and _____ inches high.

   A.   144; 12   B.   84; 7   C.   72; 12   D.   60; 8

19.   According to the above passage, the LEAST accurate of the following statements is: 19.____

   A.   Gasoline may be sold from a dispensing device other than a pump.
   B.   If two different pumps are used to sell the same grade of gasoline, a price sign must appear on each pump.
   C.   The amount of governmental tax and the price of the gasoline must not be stated on the same sign.
   D.   The sizes of the numbers used on a sign to indicate the price of gasoline must be the same.

Questions 20-21.

DIRECTIONS: Questions 20 and 21 are to be answered SOLELY on the basis of the following passage.

   In all systems of weights and measures based on one or more arbitrary fundamental units, the concrete representation of the unit in the form of a standard is necessary, and the construction and preservation of such a standard is a matter of primary importance. There-fore, it is essential that the standard should be so constructed as to be as nearly permanent and invariable as human ingenuity can contrive. The reference of all measures to an original standard is essential for their correctness, and such a standard must be maintained and pre-served in its integrity by some responsible authority which is thus able to provide against the use of false weights and measures. Accordingly, from earliest times, standards were con-structed and preserved under the direction of kings and priests, and the temples were a favorite place for their deposit. Later, this duty was assumed by the government, and today we find the integrity of standards of weights and measures safeguarded by international agreement.

20.   Of the following, the MOST valid implication which can be made on the basis of the   20.____
above passage is that

   A.   fundamental units of systems of weights and measures should be represented by quantities so constructed that they are specific and constant
   B.   in the earliest times, standards were so constructed that they were as permanent and invariable as modern ones
   C.   international agreement has practically relieved the U.S. government of the neces-sity of preserving standards of weights and measures
   D.   the preservation of standards is of less importance than the ingenuity used in their construction

21. Of the following, the MOST appropriate title for the above passage is

  A. THE CONSTRUCTION AND PRESERVATION OF STANDARDS OF WEIGHTS AND MEASURES
  B. THE FIXING OF RESPONSIBILITY FOR THE ESTABLISHMENT OF STANDARDS OF WEIGHTS AND MEASURES
  C. THE HISTORY OF SYSTEMS OF WEIGHTS AND MEASURES
  D. THE VALUE OF PROPER STANDARDS IN PROVIDING CORRECT WEIGHTS AND MEASURES

Questions 22-23.

DIRECTIONS: Questions 22 and 23 are to be answered SOLELY on the basis of the following passage.

Accurate weighing and good scales insure that excess is not given just for the sake of good measure. No more striking example of the fundamental importance of correct weighing to the business man is found than in the simple and usual relation where a charge or value is obtained by multiplying a weight by a unit price. For example, a scale may weigh *light,* that is, the actual quantity delivered is in excess by 1 percent. The actual result is that the seller taxes himself. If his profit is supposed to be 10 percent of total sales, an overweight of 1 percent represents 10 percent of that profit. Under these conditions, the situation is as though the seller were required to pay a sales tax equivalent to what he is taxing himself.

22. Of the following, the MOST valid implication which can be made on the basis of the above passage is that

  A. consistent use of scales that weigh *light* will reduce sellers' profits
  B. no good businessman would give any buyer more than the weight required even if his scale is accurate
  C. the kind of situation described in the above passage could not arise if sales were being made of merchandise sold by the yard
  D. the use of incorrect scales is one of the reasons causing governments to impose sales taxes

23. According to the above passage, the MOST accurate of the following statements is:

  A. If his scale weighs *light* by an amount of 2 percent, the seller would deliver only 98 pounds when 100 pounds was the amount agreed upon.
  B. If the seller's scale weighs *heavy,* the buyer will receive an amount in excess of what he intended to purchase.
  C. If the seller's scale weighs *light* by an amount of 1 percent, a buyer who agreed to purchase 50 pounds of merchandise would actually receive $50 \frac{1}{2}$ pounds.
  D. The use of a scale which delivers an amount which is in excess of that required is an example of deliberate fraud.

Questions 24-25.

DIRECTIONS: Questions 24 and 25 are to be answered SOLELY on the basis of the following passage.

Food shall be deemed to be misbranded:
1. If its labeling is false or misleading in any particular.

2. If any word, statement, or other information required by or under authority of this article to appear on the label or labeling is not prominently placed thereon with such conspicuousness (as compared with other words, statements, designs, or devices in the labeling) and in such terms as to render it likely to be read and understood by the ordinary individual under customary conditions of purchase and use.

3. If it purports to be or is represented as a food for which a standard of quality has been prescribed and its quality falls below such standard, unless its label bears a statement that it falls below such standard.

24. According to the above passage, the MOST accurate of the following statements is: 24._____

A. A food may be considered misbranded if the label contains a considerable amount of information which is not required.
B. If a consumer purchased one type of canned food, although he intended to buy another, the food is probably misbranded.
C. If a food is used in large amounts by a group of people of certain foreign origin, it can be considered misbranded unless the label is in the foreign language with which they are familiar.
D. The required information on a label is likely to be in larger print than other information which may appear on it.

25. According to the above passage, the one of the following foods which may be considered 25._____
to be misbranded is a

A. can of peaches with a label which carries the brand name of the packer but states *Below Standard in Quality*
B. can of vegetables with a label on which is printed a shield which states *U.S. Grade B*
C. package of frozen food which has some pertinent information printed on it in very small type which a customer cannot read and which the store manager cannot read when asked to do so by the customer
D. package of margarine of the same size as the usual package of butter, kept near the butter, but clearly labeled as margarine

KEY (CORRECT ANSWERS)

1.	C	11.	C
2.	D	12.	A
3.	B	13.	B
4.	B	14.	A
5.	B	15.	B
6.	A	16.	D
7.	D	17.	A
8.	C	18.	C
9.	D	19.	C
10.	A	20.	A

21.	D
22.	A
23.	C
24.	D
25.	C

———

CLERICAL ABILITIES TEST

EXAMINATION SECTION
TEST 1

DIRECTIONS: Each question or incomplete statement is followed by several suggested answers or completions. Select the one that *BEST* answers the question or completes the statement. *PRINT THE LETTER OF THE CORRECT ANSWER IN THE SPACE AT THE RIGHT.*

Questions 1-10.

DIRECTIONS: Questions 1 through 10 consist of lines of names, dates and numbers. For each question, you are to choose the option (A, B, C, or D) in Column II which *EXACTLY* matches the information in Column I. *PRINT THE LETTER OF THE CORRECT ANSWER IN THE SPACE AT THE RIGHT.*

SAMPLE QUESTION

Column I	Column II		
Schneider 11/16/75 581932	A. Schneider	11/16/75	518932
	B. Schneider	11/16/75	581932
	C. Schnieder	11/16/75	581932
	D. Shnieder	11/16/75	518932

The correct answer is B. Only option B shows the name, date and number exactly as they are in Column I. Option A has a mistake in the number. Option C has a mistake in the name. Option D has a mistake in the name and in the number. Now answer Questions 1 through 10 in the same manner.

Column I   Column II

1. Johnston 12/26/74 659251   A. Johnson 12/23/74 659251   1.____
                                  B. Johston 12/26/74 659251
                                  C. Johnston 12/26/74 695251
                                  D. Johnston 12/26/74 659251

2. Allison 1/26/75 9939256   A. Allison 1/26/75 9939256   2.____
                                  B. Alisson 1/26/75 9939256
                                  C. Allison 1/26/76 9399256
                                  D. Allison 1/26/75 9993256

3. Farrell 2/12/75 361251   A. Farell 2/21/75 361251   3.____
                                  B. Farrell 2/12/75 361251
                                  C. Farrell 2/21/75 361251
                                  D. Farrell 2/12/75 361151

4. Guerrero 4/28/72 105689   A. Guererro 4/28/72 105689   4.____
                                  B. Guererro 4/28/72 105986
                                  C. Guerrero 4/28/72 105869
                                  D. Guerrero 4/28/72 105689

5. McDonnell 6/05/73 478215

    A. McDonnell 6/15/73 478215
    B. McDonnell 6/05/73 478215
    C. McDonnell 6/05/73 472815
    D. MacDonell 6/05/73 478215

    5

6. Shepard 3/31/71 075421

    A. Sheperd 3/31/71 075421
    B. Shepard 3/13/71 075421
    C. Shepard 3/31/71 075421
    D. Shepard 3/13/71 075241

    6

7. Russell 4/01/69 031429

    A. Russell 4/01/69 031429
    B. Russell 4/10/69 034129
    C. Russell 4/10/69 031429
    D. Russell 4/01/69 034129

    7

8. Phillips 10/16/68 961042

    A. Philipps 10/16/68 961042
    B. Phillips 10/16/68 960142
    C. Phillips 10/16/68 961042
    D. Philipps 10/16/68 916042

    8

9. Campbell 11/21/72 624856

    A. Campbell 11/21/72 624856
    B. Campbell 11/21/72 624586
    C. Campbell 11/21/72 624686
    D. Campbel 11/21/72 624856

    9

10. Patterson 9/18/71 76199176

    A. Patterson 9/18/72 76191976
    B. Patterson 9/18/71 76199176
    C. Patterson 9/18/72 76199176
    D. Patterson 9/18/71 76919176

    10

Questions 11-15.

DIRECTIONS: Questions 11 through 15 consist of groups of numbers and letters which you are to compare. For each question, you are to choose the option (A, B, C, or D) in Column II which *EXACTLY* matches the group of numbers and letters given in Column I.

SAMPLE QUESTION

Column I
B92466

Column II
A. B92644
B. B94266
C. A92466
D. B92466

The correct answer is D. Only option D in Column II shows the group of numbers and letters *EXACTLY* as it appears in Column I. Now answer Questions 11 through 15 in the same manner.

Column I
11.   925AC5

Column II
A. 952CA5
B. 925AC5
C. 952AC5
D. 925CA6

12.   Y006925   A. Y060925
                                                          B. Y006295
                                                          C. Y006529
                                                          D. Y006925

13.   J236956   A. J236956
                                                          B. J326965
                                                          C. J239656
                                                          D. J932656

14.   AB6952   A. AB6952
                                                          B. AB9625
                                                          C. AB9652
                                                          D. AB6925

15.   X259361   A. X529361
                                                          B. X259631
                                                          C. X523961
                                                          D. X259361

Questions 16-25.

DIRECTIONS: Each of Questions 16 through 25 consists of three lines of code letters and
              three lines of numbers. The numbers on each line should correspond with the
              code letters on the same line in accordance with the table below.

Code Letter	S	V	W	A	Q	M	X	E	G	K
Corresponding Number	0	1	2	3	4	5	6	7	8	9

On some of the lines, an error exists in the coding. Compare the letters and numbers in each
question carefully. If you find an error or errors on:
    only *one* of the lines in the question, mark your answer A;
    any *two* lines in the question, mark your answer B;
    all *three* lines in the question, mark your answer C;
    none of the lines in the question, mark your answer D.
                         SAMPLE QUESTION
              WQGKSXG   2489068
              XEKVQMA   6591453
              KMAESXV   9527061
In the above example, the first line is correct since each code letter listed has the correct corresponding number. On the second line, an error exists because code letter E should have the
number 7 instead of the number 5. On the third line an error exists because the code letter A
should have the number 3 instead of the number 2. Since there are errors in two of the three
lines, the correct answer is B. Now answer Questions 16 through 25 in the same manner.

16.   SWQEKGA   0247983   16.____
      KEAVSXM   9731065
      SSAXGKQ   0036894

17.   QAMKMVS   4259510   17.____
      MGGEASX   5897306
      KSWMKWS   9125920

18.	WKXQWVE	2964217	18.
	QKXXQVA	4966413	
	AWMXGVS	3253810	

19.	GMMKASE	8559307	19.
	AWVSKSW	3210902	
	QAVSVGK	4310189	

20.	XGKQSMK	6894049	20.
	QSVKEAS	4019730	
	GSMXKMV	8057951	

21.	AEKMWSG	3195208	21.
	MKQSVQK	5940149	
	XGQAEVW	6843712	

22.	XGMKAVS	6858310	22.
	SKMAWEQ	0953174	
	GVMEQSA	8167403	

23.	VQSKAVE	1489317	23.
	WQGKAEM	2489375	
	MEGKAWQ	5689324	

24.	XMQVSKG	6541098	24.
	QMEKEWS	4579720	
	KMEVKGA	9571983	

25.	GKVAMEW	8912572	25
	AXMVKAE	3651937	
	KWAGMAV	9238531	

Questions 26-35.

DIRECTIONS: Each of Questions 26 through 35 consists of a column of figures. For each question, add the column of figures and choose the correct answer from the four choices given.

26. 5,665.43
2,356.69
6,447.24
7,239.65

A. 20,698.01   B. 21,709.01
C. 21,718.01   D. 22,609.01

27. 817,209.55
264,354.29
82,368.76
849,964.89

A. 1,893,997.49   B. 1,989,988.39
C. 2,009,077.39   D. 2,013,897,49

28. 156,366.89
249,973.23
823,229.49
<u>56,869.45</u>

   A. 1,286,439.06   B. 1,287,521.06
   C. 1,297,539.06   D. 1,296,421.06

28._____

29.   23,422.15
149,696.24
238,377.53
  86,289.79
<u>505,544.63</u>

   A. 989,229.34   B. 999,879.34
   C. 1,003,330.34   D. 1,023,329.34

29._____

30. 2,468,926.70
  656,842.28
   49,723.15
<u> 832,369.59</u>

   A. 3,218,061.72   B. 3,808,092.72
   C. 4,007,861.72   D. 4,818,192.72

30._____

31.   524,201.52
7,775,678.51
8,345,299.63
40,628,898.08
<u>31,374,670.07</u>

   A. 88,646,647.81   B. 88,646,747.91
   C. 88,648,647.91   D. 88,648,747.81

31._____

32. 6,824,829.40
  682,482.94
5,542,015.27
  775,678.51
<u>7,732,507.25</u>

   A. 21,557,513.37   B. 21,567,513.37
   C. 22,567,503.37   D. 22,567,513.37

32._____

33. 22,109,405.58
  6,097,093.43
  5,050,073.99
  8,118,050.05
<u> 4,313,980.82</u>

   A. 45,688,593.87   B. 45,688,603.87
   C. 45,689,593.87   D. 45,689,603.87

33._____

34. 79,324,114.19
99,848,129.74
43,331,653.31
<u>41,610,207.14</u>

34._____

A. 264,114,104.38   B. 264,114,114.38
C. 265,114,114.38   D. 265,214,104.38

35.   33,729,653.94
        5,959,342.58
       26,052,715.47
        4,452,669.52
        7,079,953.59

A. 76,374,334.10   B. 76,375,334.10
C. 77,274,335.10   D. 77,275,335.10

Questions 36-40.

DIRECTIONS: Each of Questions 36 through 40 consists of a single number in Column I and
               four options in Column II. For each question, you are to choose the option (A,
               B, C, or D) in Column II which *EXACTLY* matches the number in Column I.
               SAMPLE QUESTION

Column I   Column II
5965121   A.   5956121
                           B.   5965121
                           C.   5966121
                           D.   5965211

The correct answer is B. Only option B shows the number *EXACTLY* as it appears in Column I.
Now answer Questions 36 through 40 in the same manner.

Column I   Column II
36.   9643242   A.   9643242
                           B.   9462342
                           C.   9642442
                           D.   9463242

37.   3572477   A.   3752477
                          B.   3725477
                          C.   3572477
                          D.   3574277

38.   5276101   A.   5267101
                          B.   5726011
                          C.   5271601
                          D.   5276101

39.   4469329   A.   4496329
                          B.   4469329
                          C.   4496239
                          D.   4469239

40.   2326308   A.   2236308
                          B.   2233608
                          C.   2326308
                          D.   2323608

KEY (CORRECT ANSWERS)

1.	D	11.	B	21.	A	31.	D
2.	A	12.	D	22.	C	32.	A
3.	B	13.	A	23.	B	33.	B
4.	D	14.	A	24.	D	34.	A
5.	B	15.	D	25.	A	35.	C
6.	C	16.	D	26.	B	36.	A
7.	A	17.	C	27.	D	37.	C
8.	C	18.	A	28.	A	38.	D
9.	A	19.	D	29.	C	39.	B
10.	B	20.	B	30.	C	40.	C

TEST 2

Questions 1-5.

DIRECTIONS: Each of Questions 1 through 5 consists of a name and a dollar amount. In each question, the name and dollar amount in Column II should be an exact copy of the name and dollar amount in Column I. If there is:

a mistake only in the name, mark your answer A;
a mistake only in the dollar amount, mark your answer B;
a mistake in both the name and the dollar amount, mark your answer C;
no mistake in either the name or the dollar amount, mark your answer D.

SAMPLE QUESTION

Column I	Column II
George Peterson	George Petersson
$125.50	$125.50

Compare the name and dollar amount in Column II with the name and dollar amount in Column I. The name *Petersson* in Column II is spelled *Peterson* in Column I. The amount is the same in both columns. Since there is a mistake only in the name, the answer to the sample question is A.

Now answer Questions 1 through 5 in the same manner.

Column I	Column II	
1. Susanne Shultz	Susanne Schultz	1
$3440	$3440	
2. Anibal P. Contrucci	Anibel P. Contrucci	2
$2121.61	$2112.61	
3. Eugenio Mendoza	Eugenio Mendozza	3
$12.45	$12.45	
4. Maurice Gluckstadt	Maurice Gluckstadt	4
$4297	$4297	
5. John Pampellonne	John Pammpellonne	5
$4656.94	$4566.94	

Questions 6-11.

DIRECTIONS: Each of Questions 6 through 11 consists of a set of names and addresses which you are to compare. In each question, the name and addresses in Column II should be an *EXACT* copy of the name and address in Column I. If there is:

a mistake only in the name, mark your answer A;
a mistake only in the address, mark your answer B;
a mistake in both the name and address, mark your answer C;
no mistake in either the name or address, mark your answer D.

SAMPLE QUESTION

Column I	Column II
Michael Filbert	Michael Filbert
456 Reade Street	645 Reade Street
New York, N.	New York, N . Y. 10013

Since there is a mistake only in the address (the street number should be 456 instead of 645), the answer to the sample question is B.

Now answer Questions 6 through 11 in the same manner.

	Column I	Column II	
6.	Hilda Goettelmann 55 Lenox Rd. Brooklyn, N. Y. 11226	Hilda Goettelman 55 Lenox Ave. Brooklyn, N. Y. 11226	6._____
7.	Arthur Sherman 2522 Batchelder St. Brooklyn, N. Y. 11235	Arthur Sharman 2522 Batcheder St. Brooklyn, N. Y. 11253	7._____
8.	Ralph Barnett 300 West 28 Street New York, New York 10001	Ralph Barnett 300 West 28 Street New York, New York 10001	8._____
9.	George Goodwin 135 Palmer Avenue Staten Island, New York 10302	George Godwin 135 Palmer Avenue Staten Island, New York 10302	9._____
10.	Alonso Ramirez 232 West 79 Street New York, N. Y. 10024	Alonso Ramirez 223 West 79 Street New York, N. Y. 10024	10._____
11.	Cynthia Graham 149-35 83 Street Howard Beach, N. Y. 11414	Cynthia Graham 149-35 83 Street Howard Beach, N. Y. 11414	11._____

Questions 12-20.

DIRECTIONS: Questions 12 through 20 are problems in subtraction. For each question do the subtraction and select your answer from the four choices given.

12. 232,921.85
    -179,587.68

    A. 52,433.17   B. 52,434.17
    C. 53,334.17   D. 53,343.17

12._____

13. 5,531,876.29
    -3,897,158.36

    A. 1,634,717.93   B. 1,644,718.93
    C. 1,734,717.93   D. 1,734,718.93

13._____

14. 1,482,658.22
    - 937,925.76

    A. 544,633.46   B. 544,732.46
    C. 545,632.46   D. 545,732.46

14._____

15. 937,828.17
    -259,673.88

    A. 678,154.29   B. 679,154.29
    C. 688,155.39   D. 699,155.39

15._____

16. 760,412.38
     -263,465.95

    A. 496,046.43   B. 496,946.43
    C. 496,956.43   D. 497,046.43

17. 3,203,902.26
     -2,933,087.96

    A. 260,814.30   B. 269,824.30
    C. 270,814.30   D. 270,824.30

18. 1,023,468.71
     - 934,678.88

    A. 88,780.83   B. 88,789.83
    C. 88,880.83   D. 88,889.83

19. 831,549.47
     -772,814.78

    A. 58,734.69   B. 58,834.69
    C. 59,735,69   D. 59,834.69

20. 6,306,281.74
     -3,617,376.75

    A. 2,687,904.99   B. 2,688,904.99
    C. 2,689,804.99   D. 2,799,905.99

Questions 21-30.

DIRECTIONS: Each of Questions 21 through 30 consists of three lines of code letters and three lines of numbers. The numbers on each line should correspond with the code letters on the same line in accordance with the table below.

Code Letter	J	U	B	T	Y	D	K	R	L	P
Corresponding Number	0	1	2	3	4	5	6	7	8	9

On some of the lines, an error exists in the coding. Compare the letters and numbers in each question carefully. If you find an error or errors on:

only *one* of the lines in the question, mark your answer A;
any *two* lines in the question, mark your answer B;
all *three* lines in the question, mark your answer C;
none of the lines in the question, mark your answer D.

SAMPLE QUESTION

BJRPYUR   2079417
DTBPYKJ   5328460
YKLDBLT   4685283

In the above sample the first line is correct since each code letter listed has the correct corresponding number. On the second line, an error exists because code letter P should have the number 9 instead of the number 8. The third line is correct since each code letter listed has the correct corresponding number. Since there is an error in *one* of the three lines, the correct answer is A.

Now answer Questions 21 through 30 in the same manner.

21. BYPDTJL   2495308   21.____
      PLRDTJU   9815301
      DTJRYLK   5207486

22. RPBYRJK   7934706   22.____
      PKTYLBU   9624821
      KDLPJYR   6489047

23. TPYBUJR   3942107   23.____
      BYRKPTU   2476931
      DUKPYDL   5169458

24. KBYDLPL   6345898   24.____
      BLRKBRU   2876261
      JTULDYB   0318542

25. LDPYDKR   8594567   25.____
      BDKDRJL   2565708
      BDRPLUJ   2679810

26. PLRLBPU   9858291   26.____
      LPYKRDJ   8936750
      TDKPDTR   3569527

27. RKURPBY   7617924   27.____
      RYUKPTJ   7426930
      RTKPTJD   7369305

28. DYKPBJT   5469203   28.____
      KLPJBTL   6890238
      TKPLBJP   3698209

29. BTPRJYL   2397148   29.____
      LDKUTYR   8561347
      YDBLRPJ   4528190

30. ULPBKYT   1892643   30.____
      KPDTRBJ   6953720
      YLKJPTB   4860932

KEY (CORRECT ANSWERS)

1.	A		16.	B
2.	C		17.	C
3.	A		18.	B
4.	D		19.	A
5.	C		20.	B
6.	C		21.	B
7.	C		22.	C
8.	D		23.	D
9.	A		24.	B
10.	B		25.	A
11.	D		26.	C
12.	C		27.	A
13.	A		28.	D
14.	B		29.	B
15.	A		30.	D

———

CLERICAL ABILITIES
EXAMINATION SECTION

TEST 1

DIRECTIONS: Each question or incomplete statement is followed by several suggested answers or completions. Select the one that BEST answers the question or completes the statement. *PRINT THE LETTER OF THE CORRECT ANSWER IN THE SPACE AT THE RIGHT.*

Questions 1 through 4 are to be answered on the basis of the information below:

The most commonly used filing system and the one that is easiest to learn is alphabetical filing. This involves putting records in an A to Z order, according to the letters of the alphabet. The name of a person is filed by using the following order: first, the surname or last name; second, the first name; third, the middle name or initial. For example, *Henry C. Young* is filed under *Y* and thereafter under *Young, Henry C.* The name of a company is filed in the same way. For example, *Long Cabinet Co.* is filed under *L*, while *John T. Long Cabinet Co.* is filed under *L* and thereafter under *Long, John T. Cabinet Co.*

1. The one of the following which lists the names of the persons in the CORRECT alphabetical order is
    A. Mary Carrie, Helen Carrol, James Carson, John Carter
    B. James Carson, Mary Carrie, John Carter, Helen Carrol
    C. Helen Carrol, James Carson, John Carter, Mary Carrie
    D. John Carter, Helen Carrol, Mary Carrie, James Carson

1._____

2. The one of the following which lists the names of the persons in the CORRECT alphabetical order is
    A. Jones, John C.; Jones, John A.; Jones, John P.; Jones, John K.
    B. Jones, John P.; Jones, John K.; Jones, John C.; Jones, John A.
    C. Jones, John A.; Jones, John C.; Jones, John K.; Jones, John P.
    D. Jones, John K.; Jones, John C,.; Jones, John A.; Jones, John P.

2._____

3. The one of the following which lists the names of the companies in CORRECT alphabetical order is
    A. Blane Co., Blake Co., Block Co., Blear Co.
    B. Blake Co., Blane Co., Blear Co., Block Co.
    C. Block Co., Blear Co., Blane Co., Blake Co.
    D. Blear Co., Blake Co., Blane Co., Block Co.

3._____

4. You are to return to the file an index card on *Barry C. Wayne Materials and Supplies Co.* Of the following, the CORRECT alphabetical group that you should return the index card to is
    A. A to G   B. H to M   C. N to S   D. T to Z

4._____

Questions 5-10

DIRECTIONS: In each of questions 5 through 10, the names of four people are given. For each question, choose as your answer the one of the four names given which would be filed FIRST according to the usual system of alphabetical filing of names, as described in the following paragraph.

In filing names, you must start with the last name. Names are filed in order of the first letter of the last name, then the second letter, etc. Therefore, BAILY would be filed by BROWN, which would be filed before COLT. A name with fewer letters of the same type comes first; i.e., Smith before Smithe. If the last names are the same, the names are filed alphabetically by the first name. If the first name is an initial, a name with an initial would come before a first name that starts with the same letter as the initial. Therefore, I. BROWN would come before IRA BROWN. Finally, if both last name and first name are the same, the name would be filed alphabetically by the middle name, once again an initial coming before a middle name which starts with the same letter as the initial. If there is no middle name at all, the name would come before those with middle initials or names.

Sample Question:

      A. Lester Daniels
      B. William Dancer
      C. Nathan Danzig
      D. Dan Lester

The last names beginning with D are filed before the last name beginning with L. Since DANIELS, DANCER and DANZIG all begin with the same three letters, you must look at the fourth letter of the last name to determine which name should be filed first. C comes before I or Z, so DANCER is filed before DANIELS or DANZIG. Therefore, the answer to the question is B.

5. A. Scott Biala   B. Mary Byala   5._____
   C. Martin Baylor   D. Francis Bauer

6. A. Howard J. Black   B. Howard Black   6._____
   C. J. Howard Black   D. John H. Black

7. A. Theodora Garth Kingston   B. Theadore Barth Kingston   7._____
   C. Thomas Kingston   D. Thomas T. Kingston

8. A. Paulette Mary Huerta   B. Paul M. Huerta   8._____
   C. Paulette L. Huerta   D. Peter A. Huerta

9. A. Martha Hunt Morgan   B. Martin Hunt Morgan   9._____
    C. Mary H. Morgan   D. Martine H. Morgan

10. A. James T. Meerschaum   B. James M. Mershum   10._____
    C. James F. Mearshaum   D. James N. Meshum

Questions 11 through 14 are to be answered on the basis of the following information:

You are required to file various documents in file drawers which are labeled according to the following pattern:

DOCUMENTS

MEMOS			LETTERS	
File	Subject		File	Subject
84PM1	(A-L)		84PC1	(A-L)
84PM2	(M-Z)		84PC2	(M-Z)

REPORTS			INQUIRIES	
File	Subject		File	Subject
84PR1	(A-L)		84PQ1	(A-L)
84PR2	(M-Z)		84PQ2	(M-Z)

11. A letter dealing with a burglary should be filed in the drawer labeled   11._____
    A. 84PM1   B. 84PC1   C. 84PR1   D. 84PQ2

12. A report on Statistics should be found in the drawer labeled   12._____
    A. 84PM1   B. 84PC2   C. 84PR2   D. 84PQ2

13. An inquiry is received about parade permit procedures. It should be filed   13._____
    in the drawer labeled
    A. 84PM2   B. 84PC1   C. 84PR1   D. 84PQ2

14. A police officer has a question about a robbery report you filed. You   14._____
    should pull this file from the drawer labeled
    A. 84PM1   B. 84PM2   C. 84PR1   D. 84PR2

DIRECTIONS: Each of questions 15 through 22 consist of four or six numbered names. For each question, choose the option which indicates the order in which the names should be filed in accordance with the following filing instructions:

- File alphabetically according to last name, then first name, then middle initial
- File according to each successive letter within a name
- When comparing two names in which the letters in the longer name are identical to the corresponding letters in the shorter name, the shorter name is filed first
- When the last names are the same, initials are always filed before names beginning with the same letter

15. I. Ralph Robinson   II. Alfred Ross   15._____
    III. Luis Robles   IV. James Roberts

    The CORRECT filing sequence for the above names should be
          A. IV, II, I, III   B. I, IV, III, II
          C. III, IV, I, II   D. IV, I, III, II

16. I. Irwin Goodwin   II. Inez Gonzalez   16._____
    III. Irene Goodman   IV. Ira S. Goodwin
    V. Ruth I. Goldstein   VI. M.B. Goodman

    The CORRECT filing sequence for the above names should be
          A. V, II, I, IV, III, VI   B. V, II, VI, III, IV, I
          C. V, II, III, VI, IV, I   D. V, II, III, VI, I, IV

17. I. George Allan   II. Gregory Allen   17._____
    III. Gary Allen   IV. George Allen

    The CORRECT filing sequence for the above names should be
          A. IV, III, I, II   B. I, IV, II, III
          C. III, IV, I, II   D. I, III, IV, II

18. I. Simon Kauffman   II. Leo Kaufman   18._____
    III. Robert Kaufmann   IV. Paul Kauffman

    The CORRECT filing sequence for the above names should be
          A. I, IV, II, III   B. II, IV, III, I
          C. III, II, IV, I   D. I, II, III, IV

19. I.   Roberta Williams   II. Robin Wilson   19._____
    III. Roberta Wilson   IV. Robin Williams

The CORRECT filing sequence for the above names should be
    A. III, II, IV, I   B. I, IV, III, II
    C. I, II, III, IV   D. III, I, II, IV

20. I.   Lawrence Shultz   II. Albert Schultz   20._____
    III. Theodore Schwartz   IV. Thomas Schwarz
    V. Alvin Schultz   VI. Leonard Shultz

The CORRECT filing sequence for the above names should be
    A. II, V, III, IV, I, VI   B. IV, III, V, I, II, VI
    C. II, V, I, VI, III, IV   D. I, VI, II, V, III, IV

21. I.   McArdle   II. Mayer   21._____
    III. Maletz   IV. McNiff
    V. Meyer   VI. MacMahon

The CORRECT filing sequence for the above names should be
    A. I, IV, VI, III, II, V   B. II, I, IV, VI, III, V
    C. VI, III, II, I, IV, V   D. VI, III, II, V, I, IV

22. I.   Jack E. Johnson   II. R.H. Jackson   22._____
    III. Bertha Jackson   IV. J.T. Johnson
    V. Ann Johns   VI. John Jacobs

The CORRECT filing sequence for the above names should be
    A. II, III, VI, V, IV, I   B. III, II, VI, V, IV, I
    C. VI, II, III, I, V, IV   D. III, II, VI, IV, V, I

Questions 23-30

DIRECTIONS: The code table below shows 10 letters with matching numbers. For each question, there are three sets of letters. Each set of letters is followed by a set of numbers which may or may not match their correct letter according to the code table. For each question, check all three sets of letters and numbers and mark your answer:

        A. if no pairs are correctly matched
        B. if only one pair is correctly matched
        C. if only two pairs are correctly matched
        D. if all three pairs are correctly matched

CODE TABLE

T	M	V	D	S	P	R	G	B	H
1	2	3	4	5	6	7	8	9	0

Sample Question: TMVDSP – 123456
                        RGBHTM – 789011
                        DSPRGB – 256789

In the sample question above, the first set of numbers correctly matches its set of letters. But the second and third pairs contain mistakes. In the second pair, M is incorrectly matched with number 1. According to the code table, letter M should be correctly matched with number 2. In the third pair, the letter D is incorrectly matched with number 2. According to the code table, letter D should be correctly matched with number 4. Since only one of the pairs is correctly matched, the answer is B.

23.	RSBMRM	759262		23._____
	GDSRVH	845730		
	VDBRTM	349713		
24.	TGVSDR	183247		24._____
	SMHRDP	520647		
	TRMHSR	172057		
25.	DSPRGM	456782		25._____
	MVDBHT	234902		
	HPMDBT	062491		

26.	BVPTRD	936184	26._____
	GDPHMB	807029	
	GMRHMV	827032	
27.	MGVRSH	283750	27._____
	TRDMBS	174295	
	SPRMGV	567283	
28.	SGBSDM	489542	28._____
	MGHPTM	290612	
	MPBMHT	269301	
29.	TDPBHM	146902	29._____
	VPBMRS	369275	
	GDMBHM	842902	
30.	MVPTBV	236194	30._____
	PDRTMB	647128	
	BGTMSM	981232	

KEY (CORRECT ANSWERS)

1. A	11. B	21. C
2. C	12. C	22. B
3. B	13. D	23. B
4. D	14. D	24. B
5. D	15. D	25. C
6. B	16. C	26. A
7. B	17. D	27. D
8. B	18. A	28. A
9. A	19. B	29. D
10. C	20. A	30. A

TEST 2

Questions 1-10

DIRECTIONS: Questions 1 through 10 each consist of two columns, each containing four lines of names, numbers and/or addresses. For each question, compare the lines in Column I with the lines in Column II to see if they match exactly, and mark your answer according to the following instructions:
>   A. all four lines match exactly
>   B. only three lines match exactly
>   C. only two lines match exactly
>   D. only one line matches exactly

	Column I	Column II	
1.	Earl Hodgson 1409870 Shore Ave. Macon Rd.	Earl Hodgson 1408970 Schore Ave. Macon Rd.	1._____
2.	9671485 470 Astor Court Halprin, Phillip Frank D. Poliseo	9671485 470 Astor Court Halperin, Phillip Frank D. Poliseo	2._____
3.	Tandem Associates 144-17 Northern Blvd. Alberta Forchi Kings Park, NY 10751	Tandom Associates 144-17 Northern Blvd. Albert Forchi Kings Point, NY 10751	3._____
4.	Bertha C. McCormack Clayton, MO 976-4242 New City, NY 10951	Bertha C. McCormack Clayton, MO 976-4242 New City, NY 10951	4._____
5.	George C. Morill Columbia, SC 29201 Louis Ingham 3406 Forest Ave.	George C. Morrill Columbia, SD 29201 Louis Ingham 3406 Forest Ave.	5._____

6.	506 S. Elliott Pl. Herbert Hall 4712 Rockaway Pkway 169 E. 7 St.	506 S. Elliott Pl. Hurbert Hall 4712 Rockaway Pkway 169 E. 7 St.	6._____
7.	345 Park Ave. Colman Oven Corp. Robert Conte 6179846	345 Park Pl. Coleman Oven Corp. Robert Conti 6179846	7._____
8.	Grigori Schierber Des Moines, Iowa Gouverneur Hospital 91-35 Cresskill Pl.	Grigori Schierber Des Moines, Iowa Gouverneur Hospital 91-35 Cresskill Pl.	8._____
9.	Jeffery Janssen 8041071 40 Rockefeller Plaza 407 6 St.	Jeffrey Janssen 8041071 40 Rockafeller Plaza 406 7 St.	9._____
10.	5971996 3113 Knickerbocker Ave. 8434 Boston Post Rd. Penn Station	5871996 3113 Knickerbocker Ave. 8424 Boston Post Rd. Penn Station	10._____

Questions 11-14

DIRECTIONS: Questions 11 through 14 are to be answered by looking at the four groups of names and addresses listed below and then finding out the number of groups that have their corresponding numbered lines exactly the same.

	GROUP I	GROUP II
Line 1:	Richmond General Hospital	Richman General Hospital
Line 2:	Geriatric Clinic	Geriatric Clinic
Line 3:	3975 Paerdegat St.	3975 Peardegat St.
Line 4:	Loudonville, New York 11538	Londonville, New York 11538

	GROUP III	GROUP IV
Line 1:	Richmond General Hospital	Richmend General Hospital
Line 2:	Geriatric Clinic	Geriatric Clinic
Line 3:	3795 Paerdegat St.	3975 Paerdegat St.
Line 4:	Loudonville, New York 11358	Loudonville, New York 11538

11. In how many groups is line 1 exactly the same?   11._____
    A. 2   B. 3   C. 4   D. None

12. In how many groups is line 2 exactly the same?   12._____
    A. 2   B. 3   C. 4   D. None

13. In how many groups is line 3 exactly the same?   13._____
    A. 2   B. 3   C. 4   D. None

14. In how many groups is line 4 exactly the same?   14._____
    A. 2   B. 3   C. 4   D. None

Questions 15-18

DIRECTIONS: Each of questions 15 through 18 has two lists of names and addresses. Each list contains three sets of names and addresses. Check each of the three sets in the list on the right to see if they are the same as the corresponding set in the list on the left. Mark your answers as follows:
    A. if none of the sets are the same
    B. if only one of the sets is the same
    C. if only two of the sets are the same
    D. if all three of the sets are the same

15.   Mary T. Berlinger   Mary T. Berlinger   15._____
    2351 Hampton St.   2351 Hampton St.
    Monsey, NY 20117   Monsey, NY 20117

    Eduardo Benes   Eduardo Benes
    473 Kingston Avenue   473 Kingston Avenue
    Central Islip, NY 11734   Central Islip, NY 11734

    Alan Carrington Fuchs   Alan Carrington Fuchs
    17 Gnarled Hollow Road   17 Gnarled Hollow Road
    Los Angeles, CA 91635   Los Angeles, CA 91685

16.   David John Jacobson   David John Jacobson   16._____
    178 35 St. Apt. 4C   178 53 St. Apt. 4C
    New York, NY 00927   New York, NY 00927

    Ann-Marie Calonella   Ann-Marie Calonella
    7243 South Ridge Blvd.   7243 South Ridge Blvd.
    Bakersfield, CA 96714   Bakersfield, CA 96714

    Pauline M. Thompson   Pauline M. Thomson
    872 Linden Ave.   872 Linden Ave.
    Houston, Texas 70321   Houston, Texas 70321

17. Chester LeRoy Masterton   Chester LeRoy Masterson   17._____
     152 Lacy Rd.   152 Lacy Rd.
     Kankakee, Ill. 54532   Kankakee, Ill. 54532

     William Maloney   William Maloney
     S. LaCrosse Pla.   S. LaCross Pla.
     Wausau, Wisconsin 52146   Wausau, Wisconsin 52146

     Cynthia V. Barnes   Cynthia V. Barnes
     16 Pines Rd.   16 Pines Rd.
     Greenpoint, Miss. 20376   Greenpoint, Miss. 20376

18. Marcel Jean Frontenac   Marcel Jean Frontenac   18._____
     8 Burton On The Water   6 Burton On The Water
     Calender, Me. 01471   Calender, Me. 01471

     J. Scott Marsden   J. Scott Marsden
     174 S. Tipton St.   174 Tipton St.
     Cleveland, Ohio   Cleveland, Ohio

     Lawrence T. Haney   Lawrence T. Haney
     171 McDonough St.   171 McDonough St.
     Decatur, GA 31304   Decatur, GA 31304

Questions 19-26

DIRECTIONS: Each of questions 19 through 26 has two lists of numbers. Each list contains three sets of numbers. Check each of the three sets in the list on the right to see if they are the same as the corresponding set in the list on the left. Mark your answers as follows:

      A. if none of the sets are the same
      B. if only one of the sets is the same
      C. if only two of the sets are the same
      D. if all three of the sets are the same

19. 7354183476   7354983476   19._____
     4474747744   4474747774
     57914302311   57914902311

20. 7143592185   7143892185   20._____
     8344517699   8344518699
     9178531263   9178531263

21. 2572114731   257214731   21._____
     8806835476   8806835476
     8255831246   8255831246

22.	331476853821	331476858621	22._____
	6976658532996	6976655832996	
	3766042113715	3766042113745	

23.	8806663315	8806663315	23._____
	74477138449	74477138449	
	211756663666	211756663666	

24.	990006966996	99000696996	24._____
	53022219743	53022219843	
	4171171117717	4171171177717	

25.	24400222433004	24400222433004	25._____
	5300030055000355	5300030055500355	
	20000075532002022	20000075532002022	

26.	611166640660001116	61116664066001116	26._____
	7111300117001100733	7111300117001100733	
	26666446664476518	26666446664476518	

Questions 27-30

DIRECTIONS: Questions 27 through 30 are to be answered by picking the answer which is in the correct numerical order, from the lowest to highest number, in each question.

27. A. 44533, 44518, 44516, 44547   27._____
     B. 44516, 44518, 44533, 44547
     C. 44547, 44533, 44518, 44516
     D. 44518, 44516, 44547, 44533

28. A. 95587, 95593, 95601, 95620   28._____
     B. 95601, 95620, 95587, 95593
     C. 95593, 95587, 95601, 95620
     D. 95620, 95601, 95593, 95587

29. A. 232212, 232208, 232232, 232223   29._____
     B. 232208, 232223, 232212, 232232
     C. 232208, 232212, 232223, 232232
     D. 232223, 232232, 232208, 232212

30. A. 113419, 113521, 113462, 113588   30._____
     B. 113588, 113462, 113521, 113419
     C. 113521, 113588, 113419, 113462
     D. 113419, 113462, 113521, 113588

KEY (CORRECT ANSWERS)

1. C	11. A	21. C
2. B	12. C	22. A
3. D	13. A	23. D
4. A	14. A	24. A
5. C	15. C	25. C
6. B	16. B	26. C
7. D	17. B	27. B
8. A	18. B	28. A
9. D	19. B	29. C
10. C	20. B	30. D

RECORD KEEPING
EXAMINATION SECTION
TEST 1

DIRECTIONS: Each question or incomplete statement is followed by several suggested answers or completions. Select the one that BEST answers the question or completes the statement. *PRINT THE LETTER OF THE CORRECT ANSWER IN THE SPACE AT THE RIGHT.*

Questions 1-15.

DIRECTIONS: Questions 1 through 15 are to be answered on the basis of the following list of company names below. Arrange a file alphabetically, word-by-word, disregarding punctuation, conjunctions, and apostrophes. Then answer the questions.

A Bee C Reading Materials
ABCO Parts
A Better Course for Test Preparation
AAA Auto Parts Co.
A-Z Auto Parts, Inc.
Aabar Books
Abbey, Joanne
Boman-Sylvan Law Firm
BMW Autowerks
C Q Service Company
Chappell-Murray, Inc.
E&E Life Insurance
Emcrisco
Gigi Arts
Gordon, Jon & Associates
SOS Plumbing
Schmidt, J.B. Co.

1. Which of these files should appear FIRST?   1._____

    A. ABCO Parts
    B. A Bee C Reading Materials
    C. A Better Course for Test Preparation
    D. AAA Auto Parts Co.

2. Which of these files should appear SECOND?   2._____

    A. A-Z Auto Parts, Inc.
    B. A Bee C Reading Materials
    C. A Better Course for Test Preparation
    D. AAA Auto Parts Co.

3. Which of these files should appear THIRD?   3._____

    A. ABCO Parts
    B. A Bee C Reading Materials
    C. Aabar Books
    D. AAA Auto Parts Co.

4. Which of these files should appear FOURTH?

   A. Aabar Books
   B. ABCO Parts
   C. Abbey, Joanne
   D. AAA Auto Parts Co.

5. Which of these files should appear LAST?

   A. Gordon, Jon & Associates
   B. Gigi Arts
   C. Schmidt, J.B. Co.
   D. SOS Plumbing

6. Which of these files should appear between A-Z Auto Parts, Inc. and Abbey, Joanne?

   A. A Bee C Reading Materials
   B. AAA Auto Parts Co.
   C. ABCO Parts
   D. A Better Course for Test Preparation

7. Which of these files should appear between ABCO Parts and Aabar Books?

   A. A Bee C Reading Materials
   B. Abbey, Joanne
   C. Aabar Books
   D. A-Z Auto Parts

8. Which of these files should appear between Abbey, Joanne and Boman-Sylvan Law Firm?

   A. A Better Course for Test Preparation
   B. BMW Autowerks
   C. Chappell-Murray, Inc.
   D. Aabar Books

9. Which of these files should appear between Abbey, Joanne and C Q Service?

   A. A-Z Auto Parts,Inc.   B. BMW Autowerks
   C. Choices A and B   D. Chappell-Murray, Inc.

10. Which of these files should appear between C Q Service Company and Emcrisco?

   A. Chappell-Murray, Inc.   B. E&E Life Insurance
   C. Gigi Arts   D. Choices A and B

11. Which of these files should NOT appear between C Q Service Company and E&E Life Insurance?

   A. Gordon, Jon & Associates
   B. Emcrisco
   C. Gigi Arts
   D. All of the above

12. Which of these files should appear between Chappell-Murray Inc., and Gigi Arts?   12.____

    A.   CQ Service Inc. E&E Life Insurance, and Emcrisco
    B.   Emcrisco, E&E Life Insurance, and Gordon, Jon & Associates
    C.   E&E Life Insurance and Emcrisco
    D.   Emcrisco and Gordon, Jon & Associates

13. Which of these files should appear between Gordon, Jon & Associates and SOS Plumb-   13.____
ing?

    A.   Gigi Arts   B.   Schmidt, J.B. Co.
    C.   Choices A and B   D.   None of the above

14. Each of the choices lists the four files in their proper alphabetical order except   14.____

    A.   E&E Life Insurance; Gigi Arts; Gordon, Jon & Associates; SOS Plumbing
    B.   E&E Life Insurance; Emcrisco; Gigi Arts; SOS Plumbing
    C.   Emcrisco; Gordon, Jon & Associates; SOS Plumbing; Schmidt, J.B. Co.
    D.   Emcrisco; Gigi Arts; Gordon, Jon & Associates; SOS Plumbing

15. Which of the choices lists the four files in their proper alphabetical order?   15.____

    A.   Gigi Arts; Gordon, Jon & Associates; SOS Plumbing; Schmidt, J.B. Co.
    B.   Gordon, Jon & Associates; Gigi Arts; Schmidt, J.B. Co.; SOS Plumbing
    C.   Gordon, Jon & Associates; Gigi Arts; SOS Plumbing; Schmidt, J.B. Co.
    D.   Gigi Arts; Gordon, Jon & Associates; Schmidt, J.B. Co.; SOS Plumbing

16. The alphabetical filing order of two businesses with identical names is determined by the   16.____

    A.   length of time each business has been operating
    B.   addresses of the businesses
    C.   last name of the company president
    D.   none of the above

17. In an alphabetical filing system, if a business name includes a number, it should be   17.____

    A.   disregarded
    B.   considered a number and placed at the end of an alphabetical section
    C.   treated as though it were written in words and alphabetized accordingly
    D.   considered a number and placed at the beginning of an alphabetical section

18. If a business name includes a contraction (such as *don't* or *it's*), how should that word be   18.____
treated in an alphabetical filing system?

    A.   Divide the word into its separate parts and treat it as two words.
    B.   Ignore the letters that come after the apostrophe.
    C.   Ignore the word that contains the contraction.
    D.   Ignore the apostrophe and consider all letters in the contraction.

19. In what order should the parts of an address be considered when using an alphabetical   19.____
filing system?

    A.   City or town; state; street name; house or building number
    B.   State; city or town; street name; house or building number
    C.   House or building number; street name; city or town; state
    D.   Street name; city or town; state

20. A business record should be cross-referenced when a(n)

    A. organization is known by an abbreviated name
    B. business has a name change because of a sale, incorporation, or other reason
    C. business is known by a *coined* or common name which differs from a dictionary spelling
    D. all of the above

21. A geographical filing system is MOST effective when

    A. location is more important than name
    B. many names or titles sound alike
    C. dealing with companies who have offices all over the world
    D. filing personal and business files

Questions 22-25.

DIRECTIONS: Questions 22 through 25 are to be answered on the basis of the list of items below, which are to be filed geographically. Organize the items geographically and then answer the questions.

    1. University Press at Berkeley, U.S.
    2. Maria Sanchez, Mexico City, Mexico
    3. Great Expectations Ltd. in London, England
    4. Justice League, Cape Town, South Africa, Africa
    5. Crown Pearls Ltd. in London, England
    6. Joseph Prasad in London, England

22. Which of the following arrangements of the items is composed according to the policy of: *Continent, Country, City, Firm or Individual Name?*

    A. 5, 3, 4, 6, 2, 1   B. 4, 5, 3, 6, 2, 1
    C. 1, 4, 5, 3, 6, 2   D. 4, 5, 3, 6, 1, 2

23. Which of the following files is arranged according to the policy of: *Continent, Country, City, Firm or Individual Name?*

    A. South Africa. Africa. Cape Town. Justice League
    B. Mexico. Mexico City, Maria Sanchez
    C. North America. United States. Berkeley. University Press
    D. England. Europe. London. Prasad, Joseph

24. Which of the following arrangements of the items is composed according to the policy of: *Country, City, Firm or Individual Name?*

    A. 5, 6, 3, 2, 4, 1   B. 1, 5, 6, 3, 2, 4
    C. 6, 5, 3, 2, 4, 1   D. 5, 3, 6, 2, 4, 1

25. Which of the following files is arranged according to a policy of: *Country, City, Firm or Individual Name?*

    A. England. London. Crown Pearls Ltd.
    B. North America. United States. Berkeley. University Press
    C. Africa. Cape Town. Justice League
    D. Mexico City. Mexico. Maria Sanchez

26. Under which of the following circumstances would a phonetic filing system be MOST effective?   26._____

    A. When the person in charge of filing can't spell very well
    B. With large files with names that sound alike
    C. With large files with names that are spelled alike
    D. All of the above

Questions 27-29.

DIRECTIONS: Questions 27 through 29 are to be answered on the basis of the following list of numerical files.
    1. 391-023-100
    2. 361-132-170
    3. 385-732-200
    4. 381-432-150
    5. 391-632-387
    6. 361-423-303
    7. 391-123-271

27. Which of the following arrangements of the files follows a consecutive-digit system?   27._____

    A. 2, 3, 4, 1   B. 1, 5, 7, 3
    C. 2, 4, 3, 1   D. 3, 1, 5, 7

28. Which of the following arrangements follows a terminal-digit system?   28._____

    A. 1, 7, 2, 4, 3   B. 2, 1, 4, 5, 7
    C. 7, 6, 5, 4, 3   D. 1, 4, 2, 3, 7

29. Which of the following lists follows a middle-digit system?   29._____

    A. 1, 7, 2, 6, 4, 5, 3   B. 1, 2, 7, 4, 6, 5, 3
    C. 7, 2, 1, 3, 5, 6, 4   D. 7, 1, 2, 4, 6, 5, 3

Questions 30-31.

DIRECTIONS: Questions 30 and 31 are to be answered on the basis of the following information.
    1. Reconfirm Laura Bates appointment with James Caldecort on December 12 at 9:30 A.M.
    2. Laurence Kinder contact Julia Lucas on August 3 and set up a meeting for week of September 23 at 4 P.M.
    3. John Lutz contact Larry Waverly on August 3 and set up appointment for September 23 at 9:30 A.M.
    4. Call for tickets for Gerry Stanton August 21 for New Jersey on September 23, flight 143 at 4:43 P.M.

30. A chronological file for the above information would be   30

    A. 4, 3, 2, 1   B. 3, 2, 4, 1
    C. 4, 2, 3, 1   D. 3, 1, 2, 4

31. Using the above information, a chronological file for the date of September 23 would be   31

    A. 2, 3, 4   B. 3, 1, 4   C. 3, 2, 4   D. 4, 3, 2

Questions 32-34.

DIRECTIONS: Questions 32 through 34 are to be answered on the basis of the following information.
1. Call Roger Epstein, Ashoke Naipaul, Jon Anderson, and Sarah Washington on
April 19 at 1:00 P.M. to set up meeting with Alika D'Ornay for June 6 in New York.
2. Call Martin Ames before noon on April 19 to confirm afternoon meeting with Bob
Greenwood on April 20th
3. Set up meeting room at noon for 2:30 P.M. meeting on April 19th;
4. Ashley Stanton contact Bob Greenwood at 9:00 A.M. on April 20 and set up meeting for June 6 at 8:30 A.M.
5. Carol Guiland contact Shelby Van Ness during afternoon of April 20 and set up
meeting for June 6 at 10:00 A.M.
6. Call airline and reserve tickets on June 6 for Roger Epstein trip *to* Denver on July 8
7. Meeting at 2:30 P.M. on April 19th

32. A chronological file for all of the above information would be   32

    A. 2, 1, 3, 7, 5, 4, 6   B. 3, 7, 2, 1, 4, 5, 6
    C. 3, 7, 1, 2, 5, 4, 6   D. 2, 3, 1, 7, 4, 5, 6

33. A chronological file for the date of April 19th would be   33

    A. 2, 3, 7, 1   B. 2, 3, 1, 7
    C. 7, 1, 3, 2   D. 3, 7, 1, 2

34. Add the following information to the file, and then create a chronological file for April 20th: 34
8. April 20: 3:00 P.M. meeting between Bob Greenwood and Martin Ames.

    A. 4, 5, 8   B. 4, 8, 5   C. 8, 5, 4   D. 5, 4, 8

35. The PRIMARY advantage of computer records filing over a manual system is   35

    A. speed of retrieval   B. accuracy
    C. cost   D. potential file loss

KEY (CORRECT ANSWERS)

1.	B	16.	B
2.	C	17.	C
3.	D	18.	D
4.	A	19.	A
5.	D	20.	D
6.	C	21.	A
7.	B	22.	B
8.	B	23.	C
9.	C	24.	D
10.	D	25.	A
11.	D	26.	B
12.	C	27.	C
13.	B	28.	D
14.	C	29.	A
15.	D	30.	B

31.	C
32.	D
33.	B
34.	A
35.	A

CODING
EXAMINATION SECTION

COMMENTARY

An ingenious question-type called coding, involving elements of alphabetizing, filing, name and number comparison, and evaluative judgement and application, has currently won wide acceptance in testing circles for measuring clerical aptitude and general ability, particularly on the senior (middle) grades (levels).

While the directions for this question usually vary in detail, the candidate is generally asked to consider groups of names, codes, and numbers, and then, according to a given plan, to arrange codes in alphabetic order; to arrange these in numerical sequence; to re-arrange columns of names and numbers in correct order; to espy errors in coding; to choose the correct coding arrangement in consonance with the given directions and examples, etc.

This question-type appears to have few parameters in respect to form, substance, or degree of difficulty.

Accordingly acquaintance with, and practice in, the coding question is recommended for the serious candidate.

TEST 1

DIRECTIONS FOR THIS SECTION: Answer questions 1 through 8 on the basis of the code table and the instructions given below.

Code Letter for Traffic Problem	B	H	Q	J	F	L	M	I
Code Number for Action Taken	1	2	3	4	5	6	7	8

Assume that each of the capital letters on the above chart is a radio code for a particular traffic problem and that the number immediately below each capital letter is the radio code for the correct action to be taken to deal with the problem. For instance, "1" is the action to be taken to deal with problem "B", "2" is the action to be taken to deal with problem "H", and so forth.

In each question, a series of code letters is given in Column 1. Column 2 gives four different arrangements of code numbers. You are to pick the answer (A, B, C, or D) in Column 2 that gives the code numbers that match the code letters in the same order

SAMPLE QUESTION

Column 1

Column 2

BHLFMQ

A. 125678
B. 216573
C. 127653
D. 126573

According to the chart, the code numbers that correspond to these code letters are as follows: B - 1, M - 2, L - 6, F - 5, M - 7, Q - 3. Therefore, the right answer is 126573. This answer is D in Column 2.

Column 1	Column 2	
1. BHQLMI	A. 123456 B. 123567 C. 123673 D. 125678	1.____
2. HBJQLF	A. 214365 B. 213456 C. 213465 D. 214337	2.____
3. QHMLFJ	A. 321654 B. 345673 C. 327645 D. 327654	3.____
4. FLQJIM	A. 543287 B. 563487 C. 564378 D. 654378	4.____
5. FBIHMJ	A. 513274 B. 152874 C. 528164 D. 517842	5.____
6. MIHFQB	A. 872341 B. 782531 C. 782341 D. 783214	6.____
7. JLFHQIM	A. 465237 B. 456387 C. 4652387 D. 4562387	7.____
8. LBJQIFH	A. 6143852 B. 6134852 C. 61437852 D. 61431852	8.____

TEST 2

DIRECTIONS FOR THIS SECTION: Questions 1 through 5 are based on the following list showing the name and number of each of nine inmates.

1. Johnson	4. Thompson	7. Gordon
2. Smith	5. Frank	8. Porter
3. Edwards	6. Murray	9. Lopez

Each question consists of 3 sets of numbers and letters. Each set should consist of the numbers of three inmates and the first letter of each of their names. The letters should be in the same order as the numbers. In at least two of the three choices, there will be an error. On your answer sheet, mark only that choice in which the letters correspond with the numbers and are in the same order. If all three sets are wrong, mark choice D in your answer space.

SAMPLE QUESTION

    A. 386 EPM
    B. 542 FST
    C. 474 LGT

Since 3 corresponds to E for Edwards, 8 corresponds to P for Porter, and 6 corresponds to M for Murray, choice A is correct and should be entered in your answer space. Choice B is wrong because letters T and S have been reversed. Choice C is wrong because the first number, which is 4, does *NOT* correspond with the first letter of choice C, which is L. It should have been T. If choice A were also wrong, then D would be the correct answer.

1.	A. 382 EGS	B. 461 TMJ	C. 875 PLF	1.___
2.	A. 549 FLT	B. 692 MJS	C. 758 GSP	2.___
3.	A. 936 LEM	B. 253 FSE	C. 147 JTL	3.___
4.	A. 569 PML	B. 716 GJP	C. 842 PTS	4.___
5.	A. 356 FEM	B. 198 JPL	C. 637 MEG	5.___

Questions 6-10

DIRECTIONS: Answer questions 6 through 10 on the basis of the following information:

In order to make sure stock is properly located, incoming units are stored as follows:

STOCK NUMBERS	BIN NUMBERS
00100 - 39999	D30, L44
40000 - 69999	I4L, D38
70000 - 99999	41L, 80D
100000 and over	614, 83D

Using the above table, choose the answer A,B,C,or D, which lists the correct Bin Number for the Stock Number given

6. 17243
   A. 41L   B. 83D   C. I4L   D. D30   6._

7. 9219
   A. D38   B. L44   C. 614   D. 41L   7._

8. 90125
   A. 41L   B. 614   C. D38   D. D30   8._

9. 10001
   A. L44   B. D38   C. 80D   D. 83D   9._

10. 200100
    A. 41L   B. I4L   C. 83D   D. D30   10._

———

TEST 3

DIRECTIONS FOR THIS SECTION: Assume that the Police Department is planning to conduct a statistical study of individuals who have been convicted of crimes during a certain year. For the purpose of this study, identification numbers are being assigned to individuals in the following manner:

4

The first two digits indicate the age of the individual:

The third digit indicates the sex of the individual:
      1. male
      2. female

The fourth digit indicates the type of crime involved:
      1. criminal homicide
      2. forcible rape
      3. robbery
      4. aggravated assault
      5. burglary
      6. larceny
      7. auto theft
      8. other

The fifth and sixth digits indicate the month in which the conviction occurred:
      01. January
      02. February, etc.

Answer questions 1 through 9 *SOLELY* on the basis of the above information and the following list of individuals and identification numbers.

Abbott, Richard	271304	Morris, Chris	212705
Collins, Terry	352111	Owens, William	231412
Elders, Edward	191207	Parker, Leonard	291807
George, Linda	182809	Robinson, Charles	311102
Hill, Leslie	251702	Sands, Jean	202610
Jones, Jackie	301106	Smith, Michael	421308
Lewis, Edith	402406	Turner, Donald	191601
Mack, Helen	332509	White, Barbara	242803

1.   The number of women on the above list is   1.____
     A. 6   B. 7   C. 8   D. 9

2.   The two convictions which occurred during February were   2.____
   for the crimes of
     A. aggravated assault and auto theft
     B. auto theft and criminal homicide
     C. burglary and larceny
     D. forcible rape and robbery

3.   The *ONLY* man convicted of auto theft was   3.____
     A. Richard Abbott   B. Leslie Hill
     C. Chris Morris   D. Leonard Parker

4.   The number of people on the list who were 25 years old   4.____
   or older is
     A. 6   B. 7   C. 8   D. 9

5.   The *OLDEST* person on the list is   5.____
     A. Terry Collins   B. Edith Lewis
     C. Helen Mack   D. Michael Smith

6. The two people on the list who are the same age are   6.___
   A. Richard Abbott and Michael Smith
   B. Edward Elders and Donald Turner
   C. Linda George and Helen Mack
   D. Leslie Hill and Charles Robinson

7. A 28-year-old man who was convicted of aggravated assault   7.___
   in October would have identification number
   A. 281410   B. 281509   C. 282311   D. 282409

8. A 33-year-old woman convicted in April of criminal homi-   8.___
   cide would have identification number
   A. 331140   B. 331204   C. 332014   D. 332104

9. The number of people on the above list who were convicted   9.___
   during the first six months of the year is
   A. 6   B. 7   C. 8   D. 9

Questions 10-19.
DIRECTIONS: The following is a list of patients who were referred
by various clinics to the laboratory for tests. After each
name is a patient identification number. Answer questions 10
through 19 based on the information contained in this list
and the explanation accompanying it.

The *first* digit refers to the clinic which made the referral:

1. Cardiac   6. Hematology
2. Renal   7. Gynecology
3. Pediatrics   8. Neurology
4. Opthalmology   9. Gastroenterology
5. Orthopedics

The *second digit* refers to the sex of the patient:

1. male   2. female

The *third* and *fourth digits* give the age of the patient.

The *last two digits* give the day of the month the laboratory
tests were performed.

LABORATORY REFERRALS DURING JANUARY

Adams, Jacqueline	320917		Miller, Michael	511806
Black, Leslie	813406		Pratt, William	214411
Cook, Marie	511616		Rogers, Ellen	722428
Fisher, Pat	914625		Saunders, Sally	310229
Jackson, Lee	923212		Wilson, Jan	416715
James, Linda	624621		Wyatt, Mark	321326
Lane, Arthur	115702			

6

10. According to the list, the number of women referred to   10.___
    the laboratory during January was
       A. 4   B. 5   C. 6   D. 7

11. The clinic from which the MOST patients were referred was   11.___
       A. Cardiac   B. Gynecology
       C. Opthamology   D. Pediatrics

12. The YOUNGEST patient referred from any clinic other   12.___
    than Pediatrics was
       A. Leslie Black   B. Marie Cook
       C. Arthur Lane   D. Sally Saunders

13. The number of pateints whose laboratory tests were per-   13.___
    formed on or before January 15 was
       A. 7   B. 8   C. 9   D. 10

14. The number of patients referred for laboratory tests who   14.___
    are under age 45 is
       A. 7   B. 8   C. 9   D. 10

15. The OLDEST patient referred to the clinic during January   15.___
    was
        A. Jacqueline Adams   B. Linda James
        C. Arthur Lane   D. Jan Wilson

16. The *ONLY* patient treated in the Orthopedics clinic was   16.___
       A. Marie Cook   B. Pat Fisher
       C. Ellen Rogers   D. Jan Wilson

17. A woman, age 37, was referred from the Hematology clinic to   17.___
    the laboratory. Her laboratory tests were performed on
    January 9. Her identification number would be
       A. 610937   B. 623709   C. 613790   D. 623790

18. A man was referred for lab tests from the Orthopedics   18.___
    clinic. He is 30 years old and his tests were performed
    on January 6. His identification number would be
       A. 413006   B. 510360   C. 513006   D. 513060

19. A 4 year old boy was referred from Pediatrics clinic to   19.___
    have laboratory tests on January 23. His identification
    number was
       A. 310422   B. 310423   C. 310433   D. 320403

TEST 4

DIRECTIONS FOR THIS SECTION: Questions 1 through 10 are to be
answered on the basis of the information and directions given
on the following page.

Assume that you are a Senior Stenographer assigned to the
personnel bureau of a city agency. Your supervisor has asked
you to classify the employees in your agency into the following
five groups:

A. employees who are college graduates, who are at least
   35 years of age but less than 50, and who have been
   employed by the city for five years or more;

B. employees who have been employed by the City for less
   than five years, who are not college graduates, and who
   earn at least $22,500 a year but less than $24,500;

C. employees who have been city employees for five years or
   more, who are at least 21 years of age but less than 35,
   and who are not college graduates;

D. employees who earn at least $24,500 a year but less than
   $26,000 who are college graduates, and who have been em-
   ployed by the city for less than five years;

E. employees who are not included in any of the foregoing
   groups.

NOTE: In classifying these employees you are to compute age
and period of service as of January 1, 1988. In all cases,
it is to be assumed that each employee has been employed continuously
in City service. In each question, consider only the information
which will assist you in classifying each employee. Any
information which is of no assistance in classifying an employee
should not be considered.

SAMPLE: Mr. Brown, a 29-year-old veteran, was appointed to his
present position of Clerk on June 1, 1985. He has completed
two years of college. His present salary is $23,050.

The correct answer to this sample is B, since the employee has
been employed by the city for less than five years, is not a
college graduate, and earns at least $22,500 a year but less than
$24,500.

DIRECTIONS: Questions 1 to 10 contain excerpts from the personnel
records of 10 employees in the agency. In the correspondingly
numbered space on the right print the capital letter preceding
the appropriate group into which you would place each employee.

1. Mr. James has been employed by the city since 1978, when he
   was graduated from a local college. Now 35 years of age,
   he earns $26,000 a year.   1.___

2. Mr. Worth began working in city service early in 1984. He
   was awarded his college degree in 1979, at the age of 21.
   As a result of a recent promotion, he now earns $24,500 a year. 2.___

8

Miss Thomas has been a city employee since August 1, 1983.   3.___
Her salary is $24,500 a year. Miss Thomas, who is 25 years
old, has had only three years of high school training.

Mr. Williams has had three promotions since entering city   4.___
service on January 1, 1976. He was graduated from college
with honors in 1959, when he was 20 years of age. His
present salary is $27,000 a year.

Miss Jones left college after two years of study to take an   5.___
appointment to a position in the city service paying $23,300 a
year. She began work on March 1, 1982 when she was 19 years
of age.

Mr. Smith was graduated from an engineering college with   6.___
honors in January 1983 and became a city employee three months
later. His present yearly salary is $25,810. Mr. Smith was
born in 1961.

Miss Earnest was born on May 31, 1964. Her education consisted 7.___
of four years of high school and one year of business school.
She was appointed as a typist in a city agency on June 1,
1982. Her annual salary is $23,500.

Mr. Adams, a 24-year-old clerk, began his city service on   8.___
July 1, 1984, soon after being discharged from the U.S.
Army. A college graduate, his present annual salary is $23,200.

Miss Charles attends college in the evenings, hoping to   9.___
obtain her degree in 1989, when she will be 30 years of age.
She has been a city employee since April 1983, and earns
$23,350.

Mr. Dolan was just promoted to his present position after   10.___
six years of city service. He was graduated from high school
in 1967, when he was 18 years of age, but did not go on
to college. Mr. Dolan's present salary is $23,500.

TEST 5

RECTIONS FOR THIS SECTION: Questions 1 through 4 each contain
ve numbers that should be arranged in numerical order. The
mber with the lowest numerical value should be first and
e number with the highest numerical value should be last.
ck that option which indicates the *correct* order of the
mbers.

        Examples: A. 9; 18; 14; 15; 27
                     B. 9; 14; 15; 18; 27
                     C. 14; 15; 18; 27; 9
                     D. 9; 14; 15; 27; 18

The correct answer is B, which indicates the proper arrangement of the five numbers.

1. A. 20573; 20753; 20738; 20837; 20098   1.___
    B. 20098; 20753; 20573; 20738; 20837
    C. 20098; 20573; 20753; 20837; 20738
    D. 20098; 20573; 20738; 20753; 20837

2. A. 113492; 113429; 111314; 113114; 131413   2.___
    B. 111314; 113114; 113429; 113492; 131413
    C. 111314; 113429; 113492; 113114; 131413
    D. 111314; 113114; 131413; 113429; 113492

3. A. 1029763; 1030421; 1035681; 1036928; 1067391   3.___
    B. 1030421; 1029763; 1035681; 1067391; 1036928
    C. 1030421; 1035681; 1036928; 1067391; 1029763
    D. 1029763; 1039421; 1035681; 1067391; 1036928

4. A. 1112315; 1112326; 1112337; 1112349; 1112306   4.___
    B. 1112306; 1112315; 1112337; 1112326; 1112349
    C. 1112306; 1112315; 1112326; 1112337; 1112349
    D. 1112306; 1112326; 1112315; 1112337; 1112349

TEST 6

DIRECTIONS FOR THIS SECTION: The phonetic filing system is a method of filing names in which the alphabet is reduced to key code letters. The six key letters and their equivalents are as follows:

KEY LETTERS	EQUIVALENTS
b	p, f, v
c	s, k, g, j, q, x, z
d	t
l	none
m	n
r	none

A key letter represents itself.
Vowels (a,e,i,o and u) and the letters w, h, and y are omitted.
For example, the name GILMAN would be represented as follows:
   G is represented by the key letter C.
   I is a vowel and is omitted.
   L is a key letter and represents itself.
   M is a key letter and represents itself.
   A is a vowel and is omitted.
   N is represented by the key letter M.

Therefore, the phonetic filing code for the name GILMAN is CLMM.

Answer questions 1 through 10 based on the information on the previous page.

1. The phonetic filing code for the name FITZGERALD would be
   A. BDCCRLD   B. BDCRLD   C. BDZCRLD   D. BTZCRLD

   1.____

2. The phonetic filing code CLBR may represent any one of the following names EXCEPT
   A. Calprey   B. Flower   C. Glover   D. Silver

   2.____

3. The phonetic filing code LDM may represent any one of the following names EXCEPT
   A. Halden   B. Hilton   C. Walton   D. Wilson

   3.____

4. The phonetic filing code for the name RODRIGUEZ would be
   A. RDRC   B. RDRCC   C. RDRCZ   D. RTRCC

   4.____

5. The phonetic filing code for the name MAXWELL would be
   A. MCLL   B. MCWL   C. MCWLL   D. MXLL

   5.____

6. The phonetic filing code for the name ANDERSON would be
   A. AMDRCM   B. ENDRSM   C. MDRCM   D. NDERCN

   6.____

7. The phonetic filing code for the name SAVITSKY would be
   A. CBDCC   B. CBDCY   C. SBDCC   D. SVDCC

   7.____

8. The phonetic filing code CMC may represent any one of the following names EXCEPT
   A. James   B. Jayes   C. Johns   D. Jones

   8.____

9. The *ONLY* one of the following names that could be represented by the phonetic filing code CDDDM would be
   A. Catalano   B. Chesterton   C. Cittadino   D. Cuttlerman

   9.____

10. The *ONLY* one of the following names that could be represented by the phonetic filing code LLMCM would be
    A. Ellington   B. Hallerman   C. Inslerman   D. Willingham

    10.____

11

KEY (CORRECT ANSWERS)

<u>TEST 1</u>

1. C
2. A
3. D
4. B
5. A
6. B
7. C
8. A

<u>TEST 2</u>

1. B
2. D
3. A
4. C
5. C
6. D
7. B
8. A
9. A
10. C

<u>TEST 3</u>

1. B
2. B
3. B
4. D
5. D
6. B
7. A
8. D
9. C
10. B

11. D
12. B
13. C
14. C
15. D
16. A
17. B
18. C
19. B

<u>TEST 4</u>

1. A
2. D
3. E
4. A
5. C
6. D
7. C
8. E
9. B
10. E

<u>TEST 5</u>

1. D
2. B
3. A
4. C

<u>TEST 6</u>

1. A
2. B
3. D
4. B
5. A
6. C
7. A
8. B
9. C
10. D

NAME and NUMBER COMPARISONS

COMMENTARY

This test seeks to measure your ability and disposition to do a job carefully and accurately, your attention to exactness and preciseness of detail, your alertness and versatility in discerning similarities and differences between things, and your power in systematically handling written language symbols.

It is actually a test of your ability to do academic and/or clerical work, using the basic elements of verbal (qualitative) and mathematical (quantitative) learning - words _and_ numbers.

EXAMINATION SECTION
TEST 1

DIRECTIONS: In each line across the page there are three names or numbers that are much alike. Compare the three names or numbers and decide which ones are exactly alike. _PRINT IN THE SPACE AT THE RIGHT THE LETTER:_
  A. if all THREE names or numbers are exactly ALIKE
  B. if only the FIRST and SECOND names or numbers are ALIKE
  C. if only the FIRST and THIRD names or numbers are ALIKE
  D. if only the SECOND and THIRD names or numbers are ALIKE
  E. if ALL THREE names or numbers are DIFFERENT

1.	Davis Hazen	David Hozen	David Hazen	1._____
2.	Lois Appel	Lois Appel	Lois Apfel	2._____
3.	June Allan	Jane Allan	Jane Allan	3._____
4.	10235	10235	10235	4._____
5.	32614	32164	32614	5._____

TEST 2

1.	2395890	2395890	2395890	1._____
2.	1926341	1926347	1926314	2._____
3.	E. Owens McVey	E. Owen McVey	E. Owen McVay	3._____
4.	Emily Neal Rouse	Emily Neal Rowse	Emily Neal Rowse	4._____
5.	H. Merritt Audubon	H. Merriott Audubon	H. Merritt Audubon	5._____

TEST 3

1. 6219354	6219354	6219354
2. 2312793	2312793	2312793
3. 1065407	1065407	1065047
4. Francis Ransdell	Frances Ramsdell	Francis Ramsdell
5. Cornelius Detwiler	Cornelius Detwiler	Cornelius Detwiler

TEST 4

1. 6452054	6452654	6542054
2. 8501268	8501268	8501286
3. Ella Burk Newham	Ella Burk Newnham	Elena Burk Newnham
4. Jno. K. Ravencroft	Jno. H. Ravencroft	Jno. H. Ravencoft
5. Martin Wills Pullen	Martin Wills Pulen	Martin Wills Pullen

---

TEST 5

1. 3457988	3457986	3457986
2. 4695682	4695862	4695682
3. Stricklund Kaneydy	Sticklund Kanedy	Stricklund Kanedy
4. Joy Harlor Witner	Joy Harloe Witner	Joy Harloe Witner
5. R.M.O. Uberroth	R.M.O. Uberroth	R.N.O. Uberroth

TEST 6

1.	1592514	1592574	1592574	1.____
2.	2010202	2010202	2010220	2.____
3.	6177396	6177936	6177396	3.____
4.	Drusilla S. Ridgeley	Drusilla S. Ridgeley	Drusilla S. Ridgeley	4.____
5.	Andrei I. Toumantzev	Andrei I. Tourmantzev	Andrei I. Toumantzov	5.____

TEST 7

1.	5261383	5261383	5261338	1.____
2.	8125690	8126690	8125609	2.____
3.	W.E. Johnston	W.E. Johnson	W.E. Johnson	3.____
4.	Vergil L. Muller	Vergil L. Muller	Vergil L. Muller	4.____
5.	Atherton R. Warde	Asheton R. Warde	Atherton P. Warde	5.____

TEST 8

1.	013469.5	023469.5	02346.95	1.____
2.	33376	333766	333766	2.____
3.	Ling-Temco-Vought	Ling-Tenco-Vought	Ling-Temco Vought	3.____
4.	Lorilard Corp.	Lorillard Corp.	Lorrilard Corp.	4.____
5.	American Agronomics Corporation	American Agronomics Corporation	American Agronomic Corporation	5.____

3

TEST 9

1. 436592864	436592864	436592864	1
2. 197765123	197755123	197755123	2
3. Dewaay, Cortvriendt International S.A.	Deway, Cortvriendt International S.A.	Deway, Corturiendt International S.A.	3
4. Credit Lyonnais	Credit Lyonnais	Credit Lyonais	4
5. Algemene Bank Nederland N.V.	Algamene Bank Nederland N.V.	Algemene Bank Naderland N.V.	5

TEST 10

1. 00032572	0.0032572	00032522	1
2. 399745	399745	398745	2
3. Banca Privata Finanziaria S.p.A.	Banca Privata Finanzaria S.P.A.	Banca Privata Finanziaria S.P.A.	3
4. Eastman Dillon, Union Securities & Co.	Eastman Dillon, Union Securities Co.	Eastman Dillon, Union Securities & Co.	4
5. Arnhold and S. Bleichroeder, Inc.	Arnhold & S. Bleichroeder, Inc.	Arnold and S. Bleichroeder, Inc.	5

TEST 11

DIRECTIONS: Answer the questions below on the basis of the following instructions: For each such numbered set of names, addresses and numbers listed in Columns I and II, select your answer from the following options:
- A: The names in Columns I and II are different
- B: The addresses in Columns I and II are different
- C: The numbers in Columns I and II are different
- D: The names, addresses and numbers are identical

	Column I	Column II	
1.	Francis Jones 62 Stately Avenue 96-12446	Francis Jones 62 Stately Avenue 96-21446	1.____
2.	Julio Montez 19 Ponderosa Road 56-73161	Julio Montez 19 Ponderosa Road 56-71361	2.____
3.	Mary Mitchell 2314 Melbourne Drive 68-92172	Mary Mitchell 2314 Melbourne Drive 68-92172	3.____
4.	Harry Patterson 25 Dunne Street 14-33430	Harry Patterson 25 Dunne Street 14-34330	4.____
5.	Patrick Murphy 171 West Hosmer Street 93-81214	Patrick Murphy 171 West Hosmer Street 93-18214	5.____

TEST 12

	Column I	Column II	
1.	August Schultz 816 St. Clair Avenue 53-40149	August Schultz 816 St. Claire Avenue 53-40149	1.____
2.	George Taft 72 Runnymede Street 47-04033	George Taft 72 Runnymede Street 47-04023	2.____
3.	Angus Henderson 1418 Madison Street 81-76375	Angus Henderson 1418 Madison Street 81-76375	3.____
4.	Carolyn Mazur 12 Riven/lew Road 38-99615	Carolyn Mazur 12 Rivervane Road 38-99615	4.____
5.	Adele Russell 1725 Lansing Lane 72-91962	Adela Russell 1725 Lansing Lane 72-91962	5.____

TEST 13

DIRECTIONS: The following questions are based on the instructions given below. In each of the following questions, the 3-line name and address in Column I is the master-list entry, and the 3-line entry in Column II is the information to be checked against the master list.

If there is one line that is *not* exactly alike, mark your answer A.
If there are two lines *not* exactly alike, mark your answer B.
If there are three lines *not* exactly alike, mark your answer C.
If the lines *all are* exactly alike, mark your answer D.

1.   Jerome A. Jackson   Jerome A. Johnson
        1243 14th Avenue   1234 14th Avenue
        New York, N.Y. 10023   New York, N.Y. 10023

2.   Sophie Strachtheim   Sophie Strachtheim
        33-28 Connecticut Ave.   33-28 Connecticut Ave.
        Far Rockaway, N.Y. 11697   Far Rockaway, N.Y. 11697

3.   Elisabeth NT. Gorrell   Elizabeth NT. Gorrell
        256 Exchange St   256 Exchange St.
        New York, N.Y. 10013   New York, N.Y. 10013

4.   Maria J. Gonzalez   Maria J. Gonzalez
        7516 E. Sheepshead Rd.   7516 N. Shepshead Rd.
        Brooklyn, N.Y. 11240   Brooklyn, N.Y. 11240

5.   Leslie B. Brautenweiler   Leslie B. Brautenwieler
        21-57A Seller Terr.   21-75ASeilerTerr.
        Flushing, N.Y. 11367   Flushing, N.J. 11367

KEYS (CORRECT ANSWERS)

TEST 1	TEST 2	TEST 3	TEST 4	TEST 5	TEST 6	TEST 7
1. E	1. A	1. A	1. E	1. D	1. D	1. B
2. B	2. E	2. A	2. B	2. C	2. B	2. E
3. D	3. E	3. B	3. E	3. E	3. C	3. D
4. A	4. D	4. E	4. E	4. D	4. A	4. A
5. C	5. C	5. A	5. C	5. B	5. E	5. E

TEST 8	TEST 9	TEST 10	TEST 11	TEST 12	TEST 13
1. E	1. A	1. E	1. C	1. B	1. B
2. D	2. D	2. B	2. C	2. C	2. D
3. E	3. E	3. E	3. D	3. D	3. A
4. E	4. E	4. C	4. C	4. B	4. A
5. B	5. E	5. E	5. C	5. A	5. C

NAME AND NUMBER CHECKING
EXAMINATION SECTION
TEST 1

DIRECTIONS: Each question or incomplete statement is followed by several suggested answers or completions. Select the one that *BEST* answers the question or completes the statement. *PRINT THE LETTER OF THE CORRECT ANSWER IN THE SPACE AT THE RIGHT.*

Questions 1-10

DIRECTIONS: Questions 1 through 10 below present the identification numbers, initials, and last names of employees enrolled in a city retirement system. You are to choose the option (A, B, C, or D) that has the *identical* identification number, initials, and last name as those given in each question.

SAMPLE QUESTION

B145698 JL Jones
 A. B146798 JL Jones   B. B145698 JL Jonas
 C. P145698 JL Jones   D. B145698 JL Jones

The correct answer is D. Only option D shows the identification number, initials and last name exactly as they are in the sample question. Options A, B, and C have errors in the identification number or last name.

1. J297483 PL Robinson   1._____

 A. J294783 PL Robinson   B. J297483 PL Robinson
 C. J297483 PI Robinson   D. J297843 PL Robinson

2. S497662 JG Schwartz   2._____

 A. S497662 JG Schwarz   B. S497762 JG Schwartz
 C. S497662 JG Schwartz   D. S497663 JG Schwartz

3. G696436 LN Alberton   3._____

 A. G696436 LM Alberton   B. G696436 LN Albertson
 C. G696346 LN Albertson   D. G696436 LN Alberton

4. R774923 AD Aldrich   4._____

 A. R774923 AD Aldrich   B. R744923 AD Aldrich
 C. R774932 AP Aldrich   D. R774932 AD Allrich

5. N239638 RP Hrynyk   5._____

 A. N236938 PR Hrynyk   B. N236938 RP Hrynyk
 C. N239638 PR Hrynyk   D. N239638 RP Hrynyk

6. R156949 LT Carlson   6._____

 A. R156949 LT Carlton   B. R156494 LT Carlson
 C. R159649 LT Carlton   D. R156949 LT Carlson

7. T524697 MN Orenstein 7

   A. T524697 MN Orenstein
   B. T524967 MN Orinstein
   C. T524697 NM Ornstein
   D. T524967 NM Orenstein

8. L346239 JD Remsen 8

   A. L346239 JD Remson
   B. L364239 JD Remsen
   C. L346329 JD Remsen
   D. L346239 JD Remsen

9. P966438 SB Rieperson 9

   A. P996438 SB Reiperson
   B. P966438 SB Reiperson
   C. R996438 SB Rieperson
   D. P966438 SB Rieperson

10. D749382 CD Thompson 10

    A. P749382 CD Thompson
    B. D749832 CD Thomsonn
    C. D749382 CD Thompson
    D. D749823 CD Thomspon

Questions 11 - 20

DIRECTIONS: Each of Questions 11 through 20 gives the identifi-cation number and name of a person who has received treatment at a certain hospital. You are to choose the option (A, B, C, or D) which has *EXACTLY* the same identification number and name as those given in the question.

SAMPLE QUESTION

123765 Frank Y. Jones

A. 123675 Frank Y. Jones
B. 123765 Frank T. Jones
C. 123765 Frank Y. Johns
D. 123765 Frank Y. Jones

The correct answer is D. Only option D shows the identifi-cation number and name exactly as they are in the sample question. Option A has a mistake in the identification num-ber. Option B has a mistake in the middle initial of the name. Option C has a mistake in the last name.

Now answer Questions 11 through 20 in the same manner.

11. 754898 Diane Malloy 11

    A. 745898 Diane Malloy
    B. 754898 Dion Malloy
    C. 754898 Diane Malloy
    D. 754898 Diane Maloy

12. 661818 Ferdinand Figueroa 12

    A. 661818 Ferdinand Figeuroa
    B. 661618 Ferdinand Figueroa
    C. 661818 Ferdnand Figueroa
    D. 661818 Ferdinand Figueroa

13. 100101 Norman D. Braustein 13

    A. 100101 Norman D. Braustein
    B. 101001 Norman D. Braustein
    C. 100101 Norman P. Braustien
    D. 100101 Norman D. Bruastein

14. 838696 Robert Kittredge

    A.   838969 Robert Kittredge

    B.   838696 Robert Kittredge

    C.   388696 Robert Kittredge

    D.   838696 Robert Kittridge

14.____

15. 243716 Abraham Soletsky

    A.   243716 Abrahm Soletsky

    B.   243716 Abraham Solestky

    C.   243176 Abraham Soletsky

    D.   243716 Abraham Soletsky

15.____

16. 981121 Phillip M. Maas

    A.   981121 Phillip M. Mass

    B.   981211 Phillip M. Maas

    C.   981121 Phillip M. Maas

    D.   981121 Phillip N. Maas

16.____

17. 786556 George Macalusso

    A.   785656 George Macalusso

    B.   786556 George Macalusso

    C.   786556 George Maculasso

    D.   786556 George Macluasso

17.____

18. 639472 Eugene Weber

    A.   639472 Eugene Weber

    B.   639472 Eugene Webre

    C.   693472 Eugene Weber

    D.   639742 Eugene Weber

18.____

19. 724936 John J. Lomonaco

    A.   724936 John J. Lomanoco

    B.   724396 John J. Lomonaco

    C.   724936 John J. Lomonaco

    D.   724936 John J. Lamonaco

19.____

20. 899868 Michael Schnitzer

    A.   899868 Micheal Schnitzer

    B.   898968 Michael Schnizter

    C.   899688 Michael Schnitzer

    D.   899868 Michael Schnitzer

20.____

Questions: 21 - 28

DIRECTIONS: Questions 21 through 28 consist of lines of names, dates, and numbers which represent the names. membership dates, social security numbers, and members of the retirement system. For each question you are to choose the option (A, B, C, or D) in Column II which *EXACTLY* matches the information in Column I.

SAMPLE QUESTION

Column I

Crossen 12/23/56 173568929 253492

    Column II

    A.   Crossen 2/23/56 173568929 253492

    B.   Crossen 12/23/56 173568729 253492

    C.   Crossen 12/23/56 173568929 253492

    D.   Crossan 12/23/56 173568929 258492

The correct answer is C. Only option C shows the name, date, and numbers exactly as they are in Column I. Option A has a mistake in the date. Option B has a mistake in the social security number. Option D has a mistake in the name and in the membership number.

21. Figueroa 1/15/64 119295386 147563

A.	Figueroa	1/5/64	119295386	147563
B.	Figueroa	1/15/64	119295386	147563
C.	Figueroa	1/15/64	119295836	147563
D.	Figueroa	1/15/64	119295886	147563

22. Goodridge 6/19/59 106237869 128352

A.	Goodridge	6/19/59	106287869	128332
B.	Goodrigde	6/19/59	106237869	128352
C.	Goodridge	6/9/59	106237869	128352
D.	Goodridge	6/19/59	106237869	128352

23. Balsam 9/13/57 109652382 116938

A.	Balsan	9/13/57	109652382	116938
B.	Balsam	9/13/57	109652382	116938
C.	Balsom	9/13/57	109652382	116938
D.	Balsalm	9/13/57	109652382	116938

24. Mackenzie 2/16/49 127362513 101917

A.	Makenzie	2/16/49	127362513	101917
B.	Mackenzie	2/16/49	127362513	101917
C.	Mackenzie	2/16/49	127362513	101977
D.	Mackenzie	2/16/49	127862513	101917

25. Halpern 12/2/73 115206359 286070

A.	Halpern	12/2/73	115206359	286070
B.	Halpern	12/2/73	113206359	286070
C.	Halpern	12/2/73	115206359	206870
D.	Halpern	12/2/73	115206359	286870

26. Phillips 4/8/66 137125516 192612

A.	Phillips	4/8/66	137125516	196212
B.	Philipps	4/8/66	137125516	192612
C.	Phillips	4/8/66	137125516	192612
D.	Phillips	4/8/66	137122516	192612

27. Francisce 11/9/63 123926037 152210

A.	Francisce	11/9/63	123826837	152210
B.	Francisce	11/9/63	123926037	152210
C.	Francisce	11/9/63	123936037	152210
D.	Franscice	11/9/63	123926037	152210

28.   Silbert 7/28/54 118421999 178514   28.____

A.	Silbert	7/28/54	118421999	178544
B.	Silbert	7/28/54	184421999	178514
C.	Silbert	7/28/54	118421999	178514
D.	Siblert	7/28/54	118421999	178514

KEY (CORRECT ANSWERS)

1.	B		16.	C
2.	C		17.	B
3.	D		18.	A
4.	A		19.	C
5.	D		20.	D
6.	D		21.	B
7.	A		22.	D
8.	D		23.	B
9.	D		24.	B
10.	C		25.	A
11.	C		26.	C
12.	D		27.	B
13.	A		28.	C
14.	B			
15.	D			

TEST 2

Questions 1-3

DIRECTIONS: Items 1 to 3 are a test of your proofreading ability. Each item consists of Copy I and Copy II. You are to assume that Copy I in each item is correct. Copy II, which is meant to be a duplicate of Copy I, may contain some typo-graphical errors. In each item, compare Copy II with Copy I and determine the number of errors in Copy II. If there are:

no errors, mark your answer A;
1 or 2 errors, mark your answer B;
3 or 4 errors, mark your answer C;
5 or 6 errors, mark your answer D;
7 errors or more, mark your answer E.

1.

COPY I

The Commissioner, before issuing any such license, shall cause an investigation to be made of the premises named and described in such application, to determine whether all the provisions of the sanitary code, building code, state industrial code, state minimum wage law, local laws, regulations of municipal agencies, and other requirements of this article are fully observed. (Section B32-169.0 of Article 23.)

COPY II

The Commissioner, before issuing any such license shall cause an investigation to be made of the premises named and described in such applecation, to determine whether all the provisions of the sanitary code, bilding code, state industrial code, state minimum wage laws, local laws, regulations of municipal agencies, and other requirements of this article are fully observed. (Section E32-169.0 of Article 23.)

2.

COPY I

Among the persons who have been appointed to various agencies are John Queen, 9 West 55th Street, Brooklyn; Joseph Blount, 2497 Durward Road, Bronx: Lawrence K. Eberhardt, 3194 Bedford Street, Manhattan; Reginald L. Darcy, 1476 Allerton Drive, Bronx; and Benjamin Ledwith, 177 Greene Street, Manhattan.

COPY II

Among the persons who have been appointed to various agencies are John Queen, 9 West 56th Street, Brooklyn, Joseph Blount, 2497 Dureward Road, Bronx: Lawrence K. Eberhart , 3194 Belford Street, Manhattan; Reginald L. Barcey, 1476 Allerton drive, Bronx; and Benjamin Ledwith, 177 Green Street, Manhattan.

3.

COPY I

Except as hereinafter provided, it shall be unlawful to use, store or have on hand any inflammable motion picture film in quantities greater than one standard or two sub-standard reels, or aggregating more than two thousand feet in length, or more than ten pounds in weight without the permit required by this section.

COPY II

Except as herinafter provided, it shall be unlawfull to use, store or have on hand any inflamable motion picture film, in quantities greater than one standard or two substandard reels or aggregating more than two thousand feet in length, or more then ten pounds in weight without the permit required by this section.

Questions 4-6

Questions 4 to 6 are a test of your proofreading ability. Each question consists of Copy I and Copy II. You are to assume that Copy I in each question is correct. Copy II, which is meant to be a duplicate of Copy I, may contain some typographical errors. In each question, compare Copy II with Copy I and determine the number of errors in Copy II. If there are
  no errors, mark your answer A;
  1 or 2 errors, mark your answer B;
  3 or 4 errors, mark your answer C;
  5 errors or more, mark your answer D.

4. 4.____

COPY I

It shall be unlawful to install wires or appliances for electric light, heat or power, operating at a potential in excess of seven hundred fifty volts, in or on any part of a building, with the exception of a central station, sub-station, transformer, or switching vault, or motor room; provided, however, that the Commissioner may authorize the use of radio transmitting apparatus under special conditions.

COPY II

It shall be unlawful to install wires or appliances for electric light, heat or power, operating at a potential in excess of seven hundred fifty volts, in or on any part of a building, with the exception of a central station, substation, transformer, or switching vault, or motor room, provided, however, that the Commissioner may authorize the use of radio transmitting apperatus under special conditions.

5. 5.____

COPY I

The grand total debt service for the fiscal year 2006-07 amounts to $350,563,718.63, as compared with $309,561,347.27 for the current fiscal year, or an increase of $41,002,371.36. The amount payable from other sources in 2006-07 shows an increase of $13,264,165.47, resulting in an increase of $27,733,205.89 payable from tax levy funds.

COPY II

The grand total debt service for the fiscal year 2006-07 amounts to $350,568,718.63, as compared with $309,561,347.27 for the current fiscel year, or an increase of $41,002,371.36. The amount payable from other sources in 2006-07 show an increase of $13,264,165.47 resulting in an increase of $27,733,295.89 payable from tax levy funds.

6.

COPY I

The following site proposed for the new building is approximately rectangular in shape and comprises an entire block, having frontages of about 721 feet on 16th Road, 200 feet on 157th Street, 721 feet on 17th Avenue and 200 feet on 154th Street, with a gross area of about 144,350 square feet. The 2006-07 assessed valuation is $28,700,000 of which $6,000,000 is for improvements.

COPY II

The following site proposed for the new building is approximately rectangular in shape and comprises an entire block, having frontage of about 721 feet on 16th Road, 200 feet on 157th Street, 721 feet on 17th Avenue, and 200 feet on 134th Street, with a gross area of about 114,350 square feet. The 2006-07 assessed valuation is $28,700,000 of which $6,000,000 is for improvements.

―――

KEY (CORRECT ANSWERS)

1. D
2. E
3. E
4. B
5. D
6. D

―――

TEST 3

Questions 1-8

DIRECTIONS: Each of the Questions numbered 1 through 8 consists of three sets of names and name codes. In each question, the two names and name codes on the same line are supposed to be exactly the same.

Look carefully at each set of names and codes and mark your answer

- A.   if there are mistakes in all three sets
- B.   if there are mistakes in two of the sets
- C.   if there is a mistake in only one set
- D.   if there are no mistakes in any of the sets

SAMPLE QUESTION

The following sample question is given to help you understand the procedure

Macabe, John N. - V 53162	Macade, John N. - V 53162
Howard, Joan S. - J 24791	Howard, Joan S. - J 24791
Ware, Susan B. - A 45068	Ware, Susan B. - A 45968

In the above sample question, the names and name codes of the first set are not exactly the same because of the spelling of the last name (Macabe - Macade). The names and name codes of the second set are exactly the same. The names and name codes of the third set are not exactly the same because the two name codes are different (A 45068 - A 45968). Since there are mistakes in only 2 of the sets, the answer to the sample question is B.

1.   Powell, Michael C. - 78537 F   Powell, Michael C. - 78537 F   1.____
     Martinez, Pablo J. - 24435 P   Martinez, Pablo J. - 24435 P
     MacBane, Eliot M. - 98674 E   MacBane, Eliot M. - 98674 E

2.   Fitz-Kramer Machines Inc.   Fitz-Kramer Machines Inc.   2.____
              - 259090   - 259090
     Marvel Cleaning Service   Marvel Cleaning Service
              - 482657   - 482657
     Donato, Carl G. - 637418   Danato, Carl G. - 687418

3.   Martin Davison Trading Corp.   Martin Davidson Trading Corp.   3.____
              - 43108 T   - 43108 T
     Cotwald Lighting Fixtures   Cotwald Lighting Fixtures
              - 76065 L   - 70056 L
     R. Crawford Plumbers   R. Crawford Plumbers
              - 23157 C   - 23157 G

4. Fraiman Engineering Corp.
              - M4773
    Neuman, Walter B. - N7745
    Pierce, Eric M.   - W6304

    Friaman Engineering Corp.
              - M4773
    Neumen, Walter B. - N7745
    Pierce, Eric M.   - W6304   4

5. Constable, Eugene - B 64837
    Derrick, Paul - H 27119
    Heller, Karen - S 49606

    Comstable, Eugene - B 64837
    Derrik, Paul - H 27119
    Heller, Karen - S 46906   5

6. Hernando Delivery Service Co.
              - D 7456
    Barettz Electrical Supplies
              - N 5392
    Tanner, Abraham - M 4798

    Hernando Delivery Service Co.
              - D 7456
    Barettz Electrical Supplies
              - N 5392
    Tanner, Abraham - M 4798   6

7. Kalin Associates - R 38641
    Sealey, Robert E. - P 63533
    Seals! Office Furniture
              - R 36742

    Kaline Associates - R 38641
    Sealey, Robert E. - P 63553
    Seals! Office Furniture
              - R36742   7

8. Janowsky, Philip M.- 742213
    Hansen, Thomas H. - 934816
    L. Lester and Son Inc.
              – 294568

    Janowsky, Philip M.- 742213
    Hanson, Thomas H. - 934816
    L. Lester and Son Inc.
              - 294568   8

Questions 9-13

DIRECTIONS: Each of the questions number 9 through 13 consists of three sets of names and building codes. In each question, the two names and building codes on the same line are supposed to be exactly the same.

If you find an error or errors on only *one* of the sets in the question, mark your answer A; any *two* of the sets in the question, mark your answer B; all *three* of the sets in the question, mark your answer C; *none* of the sets in the question, mark your answer D.

Column I
Duvivier, Anne P. - X52714
Dyrborg, Alfred - B4217
Dymnick, JoAnne - P482596

Column II
Duviver, Anne P. - X52714
Dyrborg, Alfred - B4267
Dymnick, JoAnne - P482596

In the above sample question, the first set of names and building codes is not exactly the same because the last names are spelled differently (Duvivier - Duviver). The second set of names and building codes is not exactly the same because the building codes are different (B4217 - B4267). The third set of names and building codes is exactly the same. Since there are mistakes in two of the sets of names and building codes, the answer to the sample question is B.

Now answer the questions on the following page using, the same procedure.

Column I	Column II	
9. Lautmann, Gerald G. - C2483 Lawlor, Michael - W44639 Lawrence, John J. - H1358	Lautmann, Gerald C. - C2483 Lawler, Michael - W44639 Lawrence, John J. - H1358	9.____
10. Mittmann, Howard - J4113 Mitchell, William T.- M75271 Milan, T. Thomas - Q67533	Mittmann, Howard - J4113 Mitchell, William T.- M75271 Milan, T. Thomas - Q67553	10.____
11. Quarles, Vincent - J34760 Quinn, Alan N. - S38813 Quinones, Peter W. - B87467	Quarles, Vincent - J34760 Quinn, Alan N. - S38813 Quinones, Peter W. - B87467	11.____
12. Daniels, Harold H. - A26554 Dantzler, Richard - C35780 Davidson, Martina - E62901	Daniels, Harold H - A26544 Dantzler, Richard - 035780 Davidson, Martin - E62901	12.____
13. Graham, Cecil J. - I20244 Granger, Deborah - T86211 Grant, Charles L. - G5788	Graham, Cecil J. - I20244 Granger, Deborah - T86211 Grant, Charles L. - G5788	13.____

KEY (CORRECT ANSWERS)

1.	D	8.	C
2.	C	9.	B
3.	A	10.	A
4.	B	11.	D
5.	A	12.	C
6.	D	13.	D
7.	B		

TEST 4

DIRECTIONS: In questions 1 to 10 there are five pairs of numbers or letters and numbers. Compare each pair and decide how many pairs are *EXACTLY ALIKE. PRINT THE LETTER OF THE CORRECT ANSWER IN THE SPACE AT THE RIGHT.*

    A. if only one pair is exactly alike
    B. if only two pairs are exactly alike
    C. if only three pairs are exactly alike
    D. if only four pairs are exactly alike
    E. if all five pairs are exactly alike

1.   73-F......F-73   FF-73. . . .FF-73
       F-7373....F-7373   373-FF...337-FF
       F-733.....337-F

2.   0-17158. . ..0-17158   0-71518 ... 0-71518
       0-11758....0-11758   0-15817... 0-15817
       0-51178....0-51178

3.   1A-7908....1A-7908   7A-8901....7A-8091
       7A-891.....7A-891   1A-9078....1A-9708.
       9A-7018....9A-7081

4.   2V-6426....2V-6246   2N-6246....2N-6246
       2V-6426....2N-6426   2N-6624....2N-6624
       2V-6462....2V-6462

5.   3NY-56......3ny-65   5NY-356.....3NY-356
       6NY-3566....3ny-3566   5NY-6536....5NY-6536
       3NY-5663....5ny-3663

6.   COB-065....COB-065   BCL-506....BCL-506
       LBC-650....LBC-650   DLB-560....DLB-560
       CDB-056....COB-065

7.   4KQ-9130....4KQ-9130   4KQ-9310....4KQ-9130
       4KQ-9031....4KQ-9031   4KQ-9301....4KQ-9301
       4KQ-9013....4KQ-9013

8.   MK-89......MK-98   98-MK......89-MK
       MSK-998........MSK-998   MOSK.......MOKS
       SMK-899....SMK-899

9.   8MD-2104....SMD-2014   2MD-8140....2MD-8140
       814-MD......814-MD   4MD-8201. . . .4MD-8201
       MD-281......MD-481

10.   161-035. .. .161-035   150-316.... 150-316
       315-160....315-160   131-650....131-650
       165-301....165-301

KEY (CORRECT ANSWERS)

1.	B	6.	D
2.	E	7.	D
3.	B	8.	B
4.	C	9.	C
5.	A	10.	E

TEST 5

DIRECTIONS: Each question or incomplete statement is followed by several suggested answers or completions. Select the one that *BEST* answers the question or completes the statement. *PRINT THE LETTER OF THE CORRECT ANSWER IN THE SPACE AT THE RIGHT.*

Questions 1-5

DIRECTIONS: Questions 1 through 5, inclusive, consist of groups of four displays representing license identification plates. Examine each group of plates and determine the number of plates in each group which are identical. Mark your answer sheets as follows:
> If only two plates are identical, mark answer A.
> If only three plates are identical, mark answer B.
> If all four plates are identical, mark answer C.
> If the plates are all different, mark answer D

EXAMPLE

| ABC123 | BCD123 | ABC123 | BCD235 |

Since only two plates are identical, the first and the third, the correct answer is A.

1.	PBV839	PVB839	PVB839	PVB839	1
2.	WTX083	WTX083	WTX083	WTX083	2
3.	B73609	D73906	BD7396	BD7906	3
4.	AK7423	AK7423	AK1423	A81324	4
5.	583Y10	683Y10	583Y01	583Y10	5

Questions 6-10

DIRECTIONS: Questions 6 through 10 consist of groups of numbers and letters similar to those which might appear on license plates. Each group of numbers and letters will be called a license identification. Choose the license identification lettered A, B, C, or D that *EXACTLY* matches the license identification shown next to the question number.

SAMPLE
NY 1977
ABC-123

A. NY 1976	B. NY 1977	C. NY 1977	D. NY 1977
ABC-123	ABC-132	CBA-123	ABC-123

The license identification given is NY 1977. The only choice
ABC-123.
that exactly matches it is the license identification next to the letter D. The correct answer is therefore D.

6.   NY 1976   6.____
                            QLT-781

A. NJ 1976	B. NY 1975	C. NY 1976	D. NY 1977
QLT-781	QLT-781	QLT-781	QLT-781

7.   FLA 1977   7.____
                            2-7LT58J

A. FLA 1977	B. FLA 1977	C. FLA 1977	D. LA 1977
2-7TL58J	2-7LTJ58	2-7LT58J	2-7LT58J

8.   NY 1975   8.____
                            OQC383

A. NY 1975	B. NY 1975	C. NY 1975	D. NY 1977
OQC383	OQC833	QCQ383	OCQ383

9.   MASS 1977   9.____
                            B-8DK02

A. MISS 1977	B. MASS 1977	C. MASS 1976	D. MASS 1977
B-8DK02	B-SDK02	B-8DK02	B-80KD2

10.   NY 1976   10.____
                            ZV0586

A. NY 1976	B. NY 1977	C. NY 1976	D. NY 1976
ZV0586	ZV0586	ZV0586	ZU0586

KEY (CORRECT ANSWERS)

1.	B	6.	C
2.	C	7.	C
3.	D	8.	A
4.	A	9.	B
5.	A	10.	C

TEST 6

DIRECTIONS: Assume that each of the capital letters in the table below represents the name of an employee enrolled in the city employees' retirement system. The number directly beneath the letter represents the agency for which the employee works, and the small letter directly beneath represents the code for the employee's account.

Name of Employee	L	O	T	Q	A	M	R	N	C
Agency	3	4	5	9	8	7	2	1	6
Account Code	r	f	b	i	d	t	g	e	n

In each of the following questions 1 through 3, the agency code numbers and the account code letters in Columns 2 and 3 should correspond to the capital letters in Column 1 and should be in the same consecutive order. For each question, look at each column carefully and mark your answer as follows:

If there are one or more errors *in Column 2 only* , mark your answer A.
If there are one or more errors *in Column 3 only,* mark your answer B.
If there are one or more errors in Column 2 and one or more errors in Column 3, mark your answer C.
If there are *NO* errors in either column, mark your answer D.
The following sample question is given to help you understand the procedure.

Column I	Column 2	Column 3
TQLMOC	583746	birtfn

In Column 2, the second agency code number (corre-sponding to letter Q) should be "9", not "8". Column 3 is coded correctly to Column 1. Since there is an error only in Column 2, the correct answer is A.

	Column 1	Column 2	Column 3
1.	Q L N R C A	9 3 1 2 6 8	i r e g n d
2.	N R M O T C	1 2 7 5 4 6	e g f t b n
3.	R C T A L M	2 6 5 8 3 7	g n d b r t

KEY (CORRECT ANSWERS)

1. D
2. C
3. B

GLOSSARY OF LEGAL TERMS

CONTENTS

GLOSSARY OF LEGAL TERMS

A

ACTION - "Action" includes a civil action and a criminal action.

A FORTIORI - A terra meaning you can reason one thing from the existence of certain facts.

A POSTERIORI - From what goes after; from effect to cause.

A PRIORI - From what goes before; from cause to effect.

AB INITIO - From the beginning.

ABATE - To diminish or put an end to.

ABET - To encourage the commission of a crime.

ABEYANCE - Suspension, temporary suppression.

ABIDE - To accept the consequences of.

ABJURE - To renounce; give up.

ABRIDGE - To reduce; contract; diminish.

ABROGATE - To annul, repeal, or destroy.

ABSCOND - To hide or absent oneself to avoid legal action.

ABSTRACT - A summary.

ABUT - To border on, to touch.

ACCESS - Approach; in real property law it means the right of the owner of property to the use of the highway or road next to his land, without obstruction by intervening property owners.

ACCESSORY - In criminal law, it means the person who contributes or aids in the commission of a crime.

ACCOMMODATED PARTY - One to whom credit is extended on the strength of another person signing a commercial paper.

ACCOMMODATION PAPER - A commercial paper to which the accommodating party has put his name.

ACCOMPLICE - In criminal law, it means a person who together with the principal offender commits a crime.

ACCORD - An agreement to accept something different or less than that to which one is entitled, which extinguishes the entire obligation.

ACCOUNT - A statement of mutual demands in the nature of debt and credit between parties.

ACCRETION - The act of adding to a thing; in real property law, it means gradual accumulation of land by natural causes.

ACCRUE - To grow to; to be added to.

ACKNOWLEDGMENT - The act of going before an official authorized to take acknowledgments, and acknowledging an act as one's own.

ACQUIESCENCE - A silent appearance of consent.

ACQUIT - To legally determine the innocence of one charged with a crime.

AD INFINITUM - Indefinitely.

AD LITEM - For the suit.

AD VALOREM - According to value.

ADJECTIVE LAW - Rules of procedure.

ADJUDICATION - The judgment given in a case.

ADMIRALTY - Court having jurisdiction over maritime cases.

ADULT - Sixteen years old or over (in criminal law).

ADVANCE - In commercial law, it means to pay money or render other value before it is due.

ADVERSE - Opposed; contrary.

ADVOCATE - (v.) To speak in favor of;
                (n.) One who assists, defends, or pleads for another.

AFFIANT - A person who makes and signs an affidavit.

AFFIDAVIT - A written and sworn to declaration of facts, voluntarily made.

AFFINITY- The relationship between persons through marriage with the kindred of each other; distinguished from consanguinity, which is the relationship by blood.

AFFIRM - To ratify; also when an appellate court affirms a judgment, decree, or order, it means that it is valid and right and must stand as rendered in the lower court.

AFOREMENTIONED; AFORESAID - Before or already said.

AGENT - One who represents and acts for another.

AID AND COMFORT - To help; encourage.

ALIAS - A name not one's true name.

ALIBI - A claim of not being present at a certain place at a certain time.

ALLEGE - To assert.

ALLOTMENT - A share or portion.

AMBIGUITY - Uncertainty; capable of being understood in more than one way.

AMENDMENT - Any language made or proposed as a change in some principal writing.

AMICUS CURIAE - A friend of the court; one who has an interest in a case, although not a party in the case, who volunteers advice upon matters of law to the judge. For example, a brief amicus curiae.

AMORTIZATION - To provide for a gradual extinction of (a future obligation) in advance of maturity, especially, by periodical contributions to a sinking fund which will be adequate to discharge a debt or make a replacement when it becomes necessary.

ANCILLARY - Aiding, auxiliary.

ANNOTATION - A note added by way of comment or explanation.

ANSWER - A written statement made by a defendant setting forth the grounds of his defense.

ANTE - Before.

ANTE MORTEM - Before death.

APPEAL - The removal of a case from a lower court to one of superior jurisdiction for the purpose of obtaining a review.

APPEARANCE - Coming into court as a party to a suit.

APPELLANT - The party who takes an appeal from one court or jurisdiction to another (appellate) court for review.

APPELLEE - The party against whom an appeal is taken.

APPROPRIATE - To make a thing one's own.

APPROPRIATION - Prescribing the destination of a thing; the act of the legislature designating a particular fund, to be applied to some object of government expenditure.

APPURTENANT - Belonging to; accessory or incident to.

ARBITER - One who decides a dispute; a referee.

ARBITRARY - Unreasoned; not governed by any fixed rules or standard.

ARGUENDO - By way of argument.

ARRAIGN - To call the prisoner before the court to answer to a charge.

ASSENT - A declaration of willingness to do something in compliance with a request.

ASSERT - Declare.

ASSESS - To fix the rate or amount.

ASSIGN - To transfer; to appoint; to select for a particular purpose.

ASSIGNEE - One who receives an assignment.

ASSIGNOR - One who makes an assignment.

AT BAR - Before the court.

AT ISSUE - When parties in an action come to a point where one asserts something and the other denies it.

ATTACH - Seize property by court order and sometimes arrest a person.

ATTEST - To witness a will, etc.; act of attestation.

AVERMENT - A positive statement of facts.

B

BAIL - To obtain the release of a person from legal custody by giving security and promising that he shall appear in court; to deliver (goods, etc.) in trust to a person for a special purpose.

BAILEE - One to whom personal property is delivered under a contract of bailment.

BAILMENT - Delivery of personal property to another to be held for a certain purpose and to be returned when the purpose is accomplished.

BAILOR - The party who delivers goods to another, under a contract of bailment.

BANC (OR BANK) - Bench; the place where a court sits permanently or regularly; also the assembly of all the judges of a court.

BANKRUPT - An insolvent person, technically, one declared to be bankrupt after a bankruptcy proceeding.

BAR - The legal profession.

BARRATRY - Exciting groundless judicial proceedings.

BARTER - A contract by which parties exchange goods for other goods.

BATTERY - Illegal interfering with another's person.

BEARER - In commercial law, it means the person in possession of a commercial paper which is payable to the bearer.

BENCH - The court itself or the judge.

BENEFICIARY - A person benefiting under a will, trust, or agreement.

BEST EVIDENCE RULE,THE - Except as otherwise provided by statute, no evidence other than the writing itself is admissible to prove the content of a writing. This section shall be known and may be cited as the best evidence rule.

BEQUEST - A gift of personal property under a will.

BILL - A formal written statement of complaint to a court of justice; also, a draft of an act of the legislature before it becomes a law; also, accounts for goods sold, services rendered, or work done.

BONA FIDE - In or with good faith; honestly.

BOND - An instrument by which the maker promises to pay a sum of money to another, usually providing that upon performances of a certain condition the obligation shall be void.

BOYCOTT - A plan to prevent the carrying on of a business by wrongful means.

BREACH - The breaking or violating of a law, or the failure to carry out a duty.

BRIEF - A written document, prepared by a lawyer to serve as the basis of an argument upon a case in court, usually an appellate court.

BURDEN OF PRODUCING EVIDENCE - The obligation of a party to introduce evidence sufficient to avoid a ruling against him on the issue.

BURDEN OF PROOF - The obligation of a party to establish by evidence a requisite degree of belief concerning a fact in the mind of the trier of fact or the court. The burden of proof may require a party to raise a reasonable doubt concerning the existence of nonexistence of a fact or that he establish the existence or nonexistence of a fact by a preponderance of the evidence, by clear and convincing proof, or by proof beyond a reasonable doubt.

Except as otherwise provided by law, the burden of proof requires proof by a preponderance of the evidence.

BUSINESS, A - Shall include every kind of business, profession, occupation, calling or operation of institutions, whether carried on for profit or not.

BY-LAWS - Regulations, ordinances, or rules enacted by a corporation, association, etc., for its own government.

C

CANON - A doctrine; also, a law or rule, of a church or association in particular.

CAPIAS - An order to arrest.

CAPTION - In a pleading, deposition or other paper connected with a case in court, it is the heading or introductory clause which shows the names of the parties, name of the court, number of the case on the docket or calendar, etc.

CARRIER - A person or corporation undertaking to transport persons or property.

CASE - A general term for an action, cause, suit, or controversy before a judicial body.

CAUSE - A suit, litigation or action before a court.

CAVEAT EMPTOR - Let the buyer beware. This term expresses the rule that the purchaser of an article must examine, judge, and test it for himself, being bound to discover any obvious defects or imperfections.

CERTIFICATE - A written representation that some legal formality has been complied with.

CERTIORARI - To be informed of; the name of a writ issued by a superior court directing the lower court to send up to the former the record and proceedings of a case.

CHANGE OF VENUE - To remove place of trial from one place to another.

CHARGE - An obligation or duty; a formal complaint; an instruction of the court to the jury upon a case.

CHARTER - (n.) The authority by virtue of which an organized body acts;
          (v.) in mercantile law, it means to hire or lease a vehicle or vessel for transportation.

CHATTEL - An article of personal property.

CHATTEL MORTGAGE - A mortgage on personal property.

CIRCUIT - A division of the country, for the administration of justice; a geographical area served by a court.

CITATION - The act of the court by which a person is summoned or cited; also, a reference to legal authority.

CIVIL (ACTIONS)- It indicates the private rights and remedies of individuals in contrast to the word "criminal" (actions) which relates to prosecution for violation of laws.

CLAIM (n.) - Any demand held or asserted as of right.

CODICIL - An addition to a will.

CODIFY - To arrange the laws of a country into a code.

COGNIZANCE - Notice or knowledge.

COLLATERAL - By the side; accompanying; an article or thing given to secure performance of a promise.

COMITY - Courtesy; the practice by which one court follows the decision of another court on the same question.

COMMIT - To perform, as an act; to perpetrate, as a crime; to send a person to prison.

COMMON LAW - As distinguished from law created by the enactment of the legislature (called statutory law), it relates to those principles and rules of action which derive their authority solely from usages and customs of immemorial antiquity, particularly with reference to the ancient unwritten law of England. The written pronouncements of the common law are found in court decisions.

COMMUTE - Change punishment to one less severe.

COMPLAINANT - One who applies to the court for legal redress.

COMPLAINT - The pleading of a plaintiff in a civil action; or a charge that a person has committed a specified offense.

COMPROMISE - An arrangement for settling a dispute by agreement.

CONCUR - To agree, consent.

CONCURRENT - Running together, at the same time.

CONDEMNATION - Taking private property for public use on payment therefor.

CONDITION - Mode or state of being; a qualification or restriction.

CONDUCT - Active and passive behavior; both verbal and nonverbal.

CONFESSION - Voluntary statement of guilt of crime.

CONFIDENTIAL COMMUNICATION BETWEEN CLIENT AND LAWYER - Information transmitted between a client and his lawyer in the course of that relationship and in confidence by a means which, so far as the client is aware, discloses the information to no third persons other than those who are present to further the interest of the client in the consultation or those to whom disclosure is reasonably necessary for the transmission of the information or the accomplishment of the purpose for which the lawyer is consulted, and includes a legal opinion formed and the advice given by the lawyer in the course of that relationship.

CONFRONTATION - Witness testifying in presence of defendant.

CONSANGUINITY - Blood relationship.

CONSIGN - To give in charge; commit; entrust; to send or transmit goods to a merchant, factor, or agent for sale.

CONSIGNEE - One to whom a consignment is made.

CONSIGNOR - One who sends or makes a consignment.

CONSPIRACY - In criminal law, it means an agreement between two or more persons to commit an unlawful act.

CONSPIRATORS - Persons involved in a conspiracy.

CONSTITUTION - The fundamental law of a nation or state.

CONSTRUCTION OF GENDERS - The masculine gender includes the feminine and neuter.

CONSTRUCTION OF SINGULAR AND PLURAL - The singular number includes the plural; and the plural, the singular.

CONSTRUCTION OF TENSES - The present tense includes the past and future tenses; and the future, the present.

CONSTRUCTIVE - An act or condition assumed from other parts or conditions.

CONSTRUE - To ascertain the meaning of language.

CONSUMMATE - To complete.

CONTIGUOUS - Adjoining; touching; bounded by.

CONTINGENT - Possible, but not assured; dependent upon some condition.

CONTINUANCE - The adjournment or postponement of an action pending in a court.

CONTRA - Against, opposed to; contrary.

CONTRACT - An agreement between two or more persons to do or not to do a particular thing.

CONTROVERT - To dispute, deny.

CONVERSION - Dealing with the personal property of another as if it were one's own, without right.

CONVEYANCE - An instrument transferring title to land.

CONVICTION - Generally, the result of a criminal trial which ends in a judgment or sentence that the defendant is guilty as charged.

COOPERATIVE - A cooperative is a voluntary organization of persons with a common interest, formed and operated along democratic lines for the purpose of supplying services at cost to its members and other patrons, who contribute both capital and business.

CORPUS DELICTI - The body of a crime; the crime itself.

CORROBORATE - To strengthen; to add weight by additional evidence.

COUNTERCLAIM - A claim presented by a defendant in opposition to or deduction from the claim of the plaintiff.

COUNTY - Political subdivision of a state.

COVENANT - Agreement.

CREDIBLE - Worthy of belief.

CREDITOR - A person to whom a debt is owing by another person, called the "debtor."

CRIMINAL ACTION - Includes criminal proceedings.

CRIMINAL INFORMATION - Same as complaint.

CRITERION (sing.)
CRITERIA (plural) - A means or tests for judging; a standard or standards.

CROSS-EXAMINATION - Examination of a witness by a party other than the direct examiner upon a matter that is within the scope of the direct examination of the witness.

CULPABLE - Blamable.

CY-PRES - As near as (possible). The rule of *cy-pres* is a rule for the construction of instruments in equity by which the intention of the party is carried out *as near as may be*, *when it* would be impossible or illegal to give it literal effect.

D

DAMAGES - A monetary compensation, which may be recovered in the courts by any person who has suffered loss, or injury, whether to his person, property or rights through the unlawful act or omission or negligence of another.

DECLARANT - A person who makes a statement.

DE FACTO - In fact; actually but without legal authority.

DE JURE - Of right; legitimate; lawful.

DE MINIMIS - Very small or trifling.

DE NOVO - Anew; afresh; a second time.

DEBT - A specified sum of money owing to one person from another, including not only the obligation of the debtor to pay, but the right of the creditor to receive and enforce payment.

DECEDENT - A dead person.

DECISION - A judgment or decree pronounced by a court in determination of a case.

DECREE - An order of the court, determining the rights of all parties to a suit.

DEED - A writing containing a contract sealed and delivered; particularly to convey real property.

DEFALCATION - Misappropriation of funds.

DEFAMATION - Injuring one's reputation by false statements.

DEFAULT - The failure to fulfill a duty, observe a promise, discharge an obligation, or perform an agreement.

DEFENDANT - The person defending or denying; the party against whom relief or recovery is sought in an action or suit.

DEFRAUD - To practice fraud; to cheat or trick.

DELEGATE (v.)- To entrust to the care or management of another.

DELICTUS - A crime.

DEMUR (v.) - To dispute the sufficiency in law of the pleading of the other side.

DEMURRAGE - In maritime law, it means, the sum fixed or allowed as remuneration to the owners of a ship for the detention of their vessel beyond the number of days allowed for loading and unloading or for sailing; also used in railroad terminology.

DENIAL - A form of pleading; refusing to admit the truth of a statement, charge, etc.

DEPONENT - One who gives testimony under oath reduced to writing.

DEPOSITION - Testimony given under oath outside of court for use in court or for the purpose of obtaining information in preparation for trial of a case.

DETERIORATION - A degeneration such as from decay, corrosion or disintegration.

DETRIMENT - Any loss or harm to person or property.

DEVIATION - A turning aside.

DEVISE - A gift of real property by the last will and testament of the donor.

DICTUM (sing.)

DICTA (plural) - Any statements made by the court in an opinion concerning some rule of law not necessarily involved nor essential to the determination of the case.

DIRECT EVIDENCE - Evidence that directly proves a fact, without an inference or presumption, and which in itself if true, conclusively establishes that fact.

DIRECT EXAMINATION - The first examination of a witness upon a matter that is not within the scope of a previous examination of the witness.

DISAFFIRM - To repudicate.

DISMISS - In an action or suit, it means to dispose of the case without any further consideration or hearing.

DISSENT - To denote disagreement of one or more judges of a court with the decision passed by the majority upon a case before them.

DOCKET (n.) - A formal record, entered in brief, of the proceedings in a court.

DOCTRINE - A rule, principle, theory of law.

DOMICILE - That place where a man has his true, fixed and permanent home to which whenever he is absent he has the intention of returning.

DRAFT (n.) - A commercial paper ordering payment of money drawn by one person on another.

DRAWEE - The person who is requested to pay the money.

DRAWER - The person who draws the commercial paper and addresses it to the drawee.

DUPLICATE - A counterpart produced by the same impression as the original enlargements and miniatures, or by mechanical or electronic re-recording, or by chemical reproduction, or by other equivalent technique which accurately reproduces the original.

DURESS - Use of force to compel performance or non-performance of an act.

E

EASEMENT - A liberty, privilege, or advantage without profit, in the lands of another.

EGRESS - Act or right of going out or leaving; emergence.

EIUSDEM GENERIS - Of the same kind, class or nature. A rule used in the construction of language in a legal document.

EMBEZZLEMENT - To steal; to appropriate fraudulently to one's own use property entrusted to one's care.

EMBRACERY - Unlawful attempt to influence jurors, etc., but not by offering value.

EMINENT DOMAIN - The right of a state to take private property for public use.

ENACT - To make into a law.

ENDORSEMENT - Act of writing one's name on the back of a note, bill or similar written instrument.

ENJOIN - To require a person, by writ of injunction from a court of equity, to perform or to abstain or desist from some act.

ENTIRETY - The whole; that which the law considers as one whole, and not capable of being divided into parts.

ENTRAPMENT - Inducing one to commit a crime so as to arrest him.

ENUMERATED - Mentioned specifically; designated.

ENURE - To operate or take effect.

EQUITY - In its broadest sense, this term denotes the spirit and the habit of fairness, justness, and right dealing which regulate the conduct of men.

ERROR - A mistake of law, or the false or irregular application of law as will nullify the judicial proceedings.

ESCROW - A deed, bond or other written engagement, delivered to a third person, to be delivered by him only upon the performance or fulfillment of some condition.

ESTATE - The interest which any one has in lands, or in any other subject of property.

ESTOP - To stop, bar, or impede.

ESTOPPEL - A rule of law which prevents a man from alleging or denying a fact, because of his own previous act.

ET AL. (alii) - And others.

ET SEQ. (sequential) - And the following.

ET UX. (uxor) - And wife.

EVIDENCE - Testimony, writings, material objects, or other things presented to the senses that are offered to prove the existence or non-existence of a fact.

Means from which inferences may be drawn as a basis of proof in duly constituted judicial or fact finding tribunals, and includes testimony in the form of opinion and hearsay.

EX CONTRACTU

EX DELICTO - In law, rights and causes of action are divided into two classes, those arising *ex contractu* (from a contract) and those arising *ex delicto* (from a delict or tort).

EX OFFICIO - From office; by virtue of the office.

EX PARTE - On one side only; by or for one.

EX POST FACTO - After the fact.

EX POST FACTO LAW - A law passed after an act was done which retroactively makes such act a crime.

EX REL. (relations) - Upon relation or information.

EXCEPTION - An objection upon a matter of law to a decision made, either before or after judgment by a court.

EXECUTOR (male)

EXECUTRIX (female) - A person who has been appointed by will to execute the will.

EXECUTORY - That which is yet to be executed or performed.

EXEMPT - To release from some liability to which others are subject.

EXONERATION - The removal of a burden, charge or duty.

EXTRADITION - Surrender of a fugitive from one nation to another.

F

F.A.S.- "Free alongside ship"; delivery at dock for ship named.

F.O.B.- "Free on board"; seller will deliver to car, truck, vessel, or other conveyance by which goods are to be transported, without expense or risk of loss to the buyer or consignee.

FABRICATE - To construct; to invent a false story.

FACSIMILE - An exact or accurate copy of an original instrument.

FACTOR - A commercial agent.

FEASANCE - The doing of an act.

FELONIOUS - Criminal, malicious.

FELONY - Generally, a criminal offense that may be punished by death or imprisonment for more than one year as differentiated from a misdemeanor.

FEME SOLE - A single woman.

FIDUCIARY - A person who is invested with rights and powers to be exercised for the benefit of another person.

FIERI FACIAS - A writ of execution commanding the sheriff to levy and collect the amount of a judgment from the goods and chattels of the judgment debtor.

FINDING OF FACT - Determination from proof or judicial notice of the existence of a fact. A ruling implies a supporting finding of fact; no separate or formal finding is required unless required by a statute of this state.

FISCAL - Relating to accounts or the management of revenue.

FORECLOSURE (sale) - A sale of mortgaged property to obtain satisfaction of the mortgage out of the sale proceeds.

FORFEITURE - A penalty, a fine.

FORGERY - Fabricating or producing falsely, counterfeited.

FORTUITOUS - Accidental.

FORUM - A court of justice; a place of jurisdiction.

FRAUD - Deception; trickery.

FREEHOLDER - One who owns real property.

FUNGIBLE - Of such kind or nature that one specimen or part may be used in the place of another.

G

GARNISHEE - Person garnished.

GARNISHMENT - A legal process to reach the money or effects of a defendant, in the possession or control of a third person.

GRAND JURY - Not less than 16, not more than 23 citizens of a county sworn to inquire into crimes committed or triable in the county.

GRANT - To agree to; convey, especially real property.

GRANTEE - The person to whom a grant is made.

GRANTOR - The person by whom a grant is made.

GRATUITOUS - Given without a return, compensation or consideration.

GRAVAMEN - The grievance complained of or the substantial cause of a criminal action.

GUARANTY (n.) - A promise to answer for the payment of some debt, or the performance of some duty, in case of the failure of another person, who, in the first instance, is liable for such payment or performance.

GUARDIAN - The person, committee, or other representative authorized by law to protect the person or estate or both of an incompetent (or of a *sui juris* person having a guardian) and to act for him in matters affecting his person or property or both. An incompetent is a person under disability imposed by law.

GUILTY - Establishment of the fact that one has committed a breach of conduct; especially, a violation of law.

H

HABEAS CORPUS - You have the body; the name given to a variety of writs, having for their object to bring a party before a court or judge for decision as to whether such person is being lawfully held prisoner.

HABENDUM - In conveyancing; it is the clause in a deed conveying land which defines the extent of ownership to be held by the grantee.

HEARING - A proceeding whereby the arguments of the interested parties are heared.

HEARSAY - A type of testimony given by a witness who relates, not what he knows personally, but what others have told hi, or what he has heard said by others.

HEARSAY RULE, THE - (a) "Hearsay evidence" is evidence of a statement that was made other than by a witness while testifying at the hearing and that is offered to prove the truth of the matter stated; (b) Except as provided by law, hearsay evidence is inadmissible; (c) This section shall be known and may be cited as the hearsay rule.

HEIR - Generally, one who inherits property, real or personal.

HOLDER OF THE PRIVILEGE - (a) The client when he has no guardian or conservator; (b) A guardian or conservator of the client when the client has a guardian or conservator; (c) The personal representative of the client if the client is dead; (d) A successor, assign, trustee in dissolution, or any similar representative of a firm, association, organization, partnership, business trust, corporation, or public entity that is no longer in existence.

HUNG JURY - One so divided that they can't agree on a verdict.

HUSBAND-WIFE PRIVILEGE - An accused in a criminal proceeding has a privilege to prevent his spouse from testifying against him.

HYPOTHECATE - To pledge a thing without delivering it to the pledgee.

HYPOTHESIS - A supposition, assumption, or toehry.

I

I.E. (id est) - That is.

IB., OR IBID.(ibidem) - In the same place; used to refer to a legal reference previously cited to avoid repeating the entire citation.

ILLICIT - Prohibited; unlawful.

ILLUSORY - Deceiving by false appearance.

IMMUNITY - Exemption.

IMPEACH - To accuse, to dispute.

IMPEDIMENTS - Disabilities, or hindrances.

IMPLEAD - To sue or prosecute by due course of law.

IMPUTED - Attributed or charged to.

IN LOCO PARENTIS - In place of parent, a guardian.

IN TOTO - In the whole; completely.

INCHOATE - Imperfect; unfinished.

INCOMMUNICADO - Denial of the right of a prisoner to communicate with friends or relatives.

INCOMPETENT - One who is incapable of caring for his own affairs because he is mentally deficient or undeveloped.

INCRIMINATION - A matter will incriminate a person if it constitutes, or forms an essential part of, or, taken in connection with other matters disclosed, is a basis for a reasonable inference of such a violation of the laws of this State as to subject him to liability to punishment therefor, unless he has become for any reason permanently immune from punishment for such violation.

INCUMBRANCE - Generally a claim, lien, charge or liability attached to and binding real property.

INDEMNIFY - To secure against loss or damage; also, to make reimbursement to one for a loss already incurred by him.

INDEMNITY - An agreement to reimburse another person in case of an anticipated loss falling upon him.

INDICIA - Signs; indications.

INDICTMENT - An accusation in writing found and presented by a grand jury charging that a person has committed a crime.

INDORSE - To write a name on the back of a legal paper or document, generally, a negotiable instrument

INDUCEMENT - Cause or reason why a thing is done or that which incites the person to do the act or commit a crime; the motive for the criminal act.

INFANT - In civil cases one under 21 years of age.

INFORMATION - A formal accusation of crime made by a prosecuting attorney.

INFRA - Below, under; this word occurring by itself in a publication refers the reader to a future part of the publication.

INGRESS - The act of going into.

INJUNCTION - A writ or order by the court requiring a person, generally, to do or to refrain from doing an act.

INSOLVENT - The condition of a person who is unable to pay his debts.

INSTRUCTION - A direction given by the judge to the jury concerning the law of the case.

INTERIM - In the meantime; time intervening.

INTERLOCUTORY - Temporary, not final; something intervening between the commencement and the end of a suit which decides some point or matter, but is not a final decision of the whole controversy.

INTERROGATORIES - A series of formal written questions used in the examination of a party or a witness usually prior to a trial.

INTESTATE - A person who dies without a will.

INURE - To result, to take effect.

IPSO FACTO - By the fact iself; by the mere fact.

ISSUE (n.) The disputed point or question in a case,

J

JEOPARDY - Danger, hazard, peril.

JOINDER - Joining; uniting with another person in some legal steps or proceeding.

JOINT - United; combined.

JUDGE - Member or members or representative or representatives of a court conducting a trial or hearing at which evidence is introduced.

JUDGMENT - The official decision of a court of justice.

JUDICIAL OR JUDICIARY - Relating to or connected with the administration of justice.

JURAT - The clause written at the foot of an affidavit, stating when, where and before whom such affidavit was sworn.

JURISDICTION - The authority to hear and determine controversies between parties.

JURISPRUDENCE - The philosophy of law.

JURY - A body of persons legally selected to inquire into any matter of fact, and to render their verdict according to the evidence.

L

LACHES - The failure to diligently assert a right, which results in a refusal to allow relief.

LANDLORD AND TENANT - A phrase used to denote the legal relation existing between the owner and occupant of real estate.

LARCENY - Stealing personal property belonging to another.

LATENT - Hidden; that which does not appear on the face of a thing.

LAW - Includes constitutional, statutory, and decisional law.

LAWYER-CLIENT PRIVILEGE - (1) A "client" is a person, public officer, or corporation, association, or other organization or entity, either public or private, who is rendered professional legal services by a lawyer, or who consults a lawyer with a view to obtaining professional legal services from him; (2) A "lawyer" is a person authorized, or reasonably believed by the client to be authorized, to practice law in any state or nation; (3) A "representative of the lawyer" is one employed to assist the lawyer in the rendition of professional legal services; (4) A communication is "confidential" if not intended to be disclosed to third persons other than those to whom disclosure is in furtherance of the rendition of professional legal services to the client or those reasonably necessary for the transmission of the communication.

General rule of privilege - A client has a privilege to refuse to disclose and to prevent any other person from disclosing confidential communications made for the purpose of facilitating the rendition of professional legal services to the client, (1) between himself or his representative and his lawyer or his lawyer's representative, or (2) between his lawyer and the lawyer's representative, or (3) by him or his lawyer to a lawyer representing another in a matter of common interest, or (4) between representatives of the client or between the client and a representative of the client, or (5) between lawyers representing the client.

LEADING QUESTION - Question that suggests to the witness the answer that the examining party desires.

LEASE - A contract by which one conveys real estate for a limited time usually for a specified rent; personal property also may be leased.

LEGISLATION - The act of enacting laws.

LEGITIMATE - Lawful.

LESSEE - One to whom a lease is given.

LESSOR - One who grants a lease

LEVY - A collecting or exacting by authority.

LIABLE - Responsible; bound or obligated in law or equity.

LIBEL (v.) - To defame or injure a person's reputation by a published writing.

(n.) - The initial pleading on the part of the plaintiff in an admiralty proceeding.

LIEN - A hold or claim which one person has upon the property of another as a security for some debt or charge.

LIQUIDATED - Fixed; settled.

LIS PENDENS - A pending civil or criminal action.

LITERAL - According to the language.

LITIGANT - A party to a lawsuit.

LITATION - A judicial controversy.

LOCUS - A place.

LOCUS DELICTI - Place of the crime.

LOCUS POENITENTIAE - The abandoning or giving up of one's intention to commit some crime before it is fully completed or abandoning a conspiracy before its purpose is accomplished.

M

MALFEASANCE - To do a wrongful act.

MALICE - The doing of a wrongful act Intentionally without just cause or excuse.

MANDAMUS - The name of a writ issued by a court to enforce the performance of some public duty.

MANDATORY (adj.) Containing a command.

MARITIME - Pertaining to the sea or to commerce thereon.

MARSHALING - Arranging or disposing of in order.

MAXIM - An established principle or proposition.

MINISTERIAL - That which involves obedience to instruction, but demands no special discretion, judgment or skill.

MISAPPROPRIATE - Dealing fraudulently with property entrusted to one.

MISDEMEANOR - A crime less than a felony and punishable by a fine or imprisonment for less than one year.

MISFEASANCE - Improper performance of a lawful act.

MISREPRESENTATION - An untrue representation of facts.

MITIGATE - To make or become less severe, harsh.

MITTIMUS - A warrant of commitment to prison.

MOOT (adj.) Unsettled, undecided, not necessary to be decided.

MORTGAGE - A conveyance of property upon condition, as security for the payment of a debt or the performance of a duty, and to become void upon payment or performance according to the stipulated terms.

MORTGAGEE - A person to whom property is mortgaged.

MORTGAGOR - One who gives a mortgage.

MOTION - In legal proceedings, a "motion" is an application, either written or oral, addressed to the court by a party to an action or a suit requesting the ruling of the court on a matter of law.

MUTUALITY - Reciprocation.

N

NEGLIGENCE - The failure to exercise that degree of care which an ordinarily prudent person would exercise under like circumstances.

NEGOTIABLE (instrument) - Any instrument obligating the payment of money which is transferable from one person to another by endorsement and delivery or by delivery only.

NEGOTIATE - To transact business; to transfer a negotiable instrument; to seek agreement for the amicable disposition of a controversy or case.

NOLLE PROSEQUI - A formal entry upon the record, by the plaintiff in a civil suit or the prosecuting officer in a criminal action, by which he declares that he "will no further prosecute" the case.

NOLO CONTENDERE - The name of a plea in a criminal action, having the same effect as a plea of guilty; but not constituting a direct admission of guilt.

NOMINAL - Not real or substantial.

NOMINAL DAMAGES - Award of a trifling sum where no substantial injury is proved to have been sustained.

NONFEASANCE - Neglect of duty.

NOVATION - The substitution of a new debt or obligation for an existing one.

NUNC PRO TUNC - A phrase applied to acts allowed to be done after the time when they should be done, with a retroactive effect.("Now for then.")

O

OATH - Oath includes affirmation or declaration under penalty of perjury.

OBITER DICTUM - Opinion expressed by a court on a matter not essentially -involved in a case and hence not a decision; also called dicta, if plural.

OBJECT (v.) - To oppose as improper or illegal and referring the question of its propriety or legality to the court.

OBLIGATION - A legal duty, by which a person is bound to do or not to do a certain thing.

OBLIGEE - The person to whom an obligation is owed.

OBLIGOR - The person who is to perform the obligation.

OFFER (v.) - To present for acceptance or rejection.

(n.) - A proposal to do a thing, usually a proposal to make a contract.

OFFICIAL INFORMATION - Information within the custody or control of a department or agency of the government the disclosure of which is shown to be contrary to the public interest.

OFFSET - A deduction.

ONUS PROBANDI - Burden of proof.

OPINION - The statement by a judge of the decision reached in a case, giving the law as applied to the case and giving reasons for the judgment; also a belief or view.

OPTION - The exercise of the power of choice; also a privilege existing in one person, for which he has paid money, which gives him the right to buy or sell real or personal property at a given price within a specified time.

ORDER - A rule or regulation; every direction of a court or judge made or entered in writing but not including a judgment.

ORDINANCE - Generally, a rule established by authority; also commonly used to designate the legislative acts of a municipal corporation.

ORIGINAL - Writing or recording itself or any counterpart intended to have the same effect by a person executing or issuing it. An "original" of a photograph includes the negative or any print therefrom. If data are stored in a computer or similar device, any printout or other output readable by sight, shown to reflect the data accurately, is an "original."

OVERT - Open, manifest.

P

PANEL - A group of jurors selected to serve during a term of the court.

PARENS PATRIAE - Sovereign power of a state to protect or be a guardian over children and incompetents.

PAROL - Oral or verbal.

PAROLE - To release one in prison before the expiration of his sentence, conditionally.

PARITY - Equality in purchasing power between the farmer and other segments of the economy.

PARTITION - A legal division of real or personal property between one or more owners.

PARTNERSHIP - An association of two or more persons to carry on as co-owners a business for profit.

PATENT (adj.) - Evident.

(n.) - A grant of some privilege, property, or authority, made by the government or sovereign of a country to one or more individuals.

PECULATION - Stealing.

PECUNIARY - Monetary.

PENULTIMATE - Next to the last.

PER CURIAM - A phrase used in the report of a decision to distinguish an opinion of the whole court from an opinion written by any one judge.

PER SE - In itself; taken alone.

PERCEIVE - To acquire knowledge through one's senses.

PEREMPTORY - Imperative; absolute.

PERJURY - To lie or state falsely under oath.

PERPETUITY - Perpetual existence; also the quality or condition of an estate limited so that it will not take effect or vest within the period fixed by law.

PERSON - Includes a natural person, firm, association, organization, partnership, business trust, corporation, or public entity.

PERSONAL PROPERTY - Includes money, goods, chattels, things in action, and evidences of debt.

PERSONALTY - Short term for personal property.

PETITION - An application in writing for an order of the court, stating the circumstances upon which it is founded and requesting any order or other relief from a court.

PLAINTIFF - A person who brings a court action.

PLEA - A pleading in a suit or action.

PLEADINGS - Formal allegations made by the parties of their respective claims and defenses, for the judgment of the court.

PLEDGE - A deposit of personal property as a security for the performance of an act.

PLEDGEE - The party to whom goods are delivered in pledge.

PLEDGOR - The party delivering goods in pledge.

PLENARY - Full; complete.

POLICE POWER - Inherent power of the state or its political subdivisions to enact laws within constitutional limits to promote the general welfare of society or the community.

POLLING THE JURY - Call the names of persons on a jury and requiring each juror to declare what his verdict is before it is legally recorded.

POST MORTEM - After death.

POWER OF ATTORNEY - A writing authorizing one to act for another.

PRECEPT - An order, warrant, or writ issued to an officer or body of officers, commanding him or them to do some act within the scope of his or their powers.

PRELIMINARY FACT - Fact upon the existence or nonexistence of which depends the admissibility or inadmissibility of evidence. The phrase "the admissibility or inadmissibility of evidence" includes the qualification or disqualification of a person to be a witness and the existence or non-existence of a privilege.

PREPONDERANCE - Outweighing.

PRESENTMENT - A report by a grand jury on something they have investigated on their own knowledge.

PRESUMPTION - An assumption of fact resulting from a rule of law which requires such fact to be assumed from another fact or group of facts found or otherwise established in the action.

PRIMA FACUE - At first sight.

PRIMA FACIE CASE - A case where the evidence is very patent against the defendant.

PRINCIPAL - The source of authority or rights; a person primarily liable as differentiated from "principle" as a primary or basic doctrine.

PRO AND CON - For and against.

PRO RATA - Proportionally.

PROBATE - Relating to proof, especially to the proof of wills.

PROBATIVE - Tending to prove.

PROCEDURE - In law, this term generally denotes rules which are established by the Federal, State, or local Governments regarding the types of pleading and courtroom practice which must be followed by the parties involved in a criminal or civil case.

PROCLAMATION - A public notice by an official of some order, intended action, or state of facts.

PROFFERED EVIDENCE - The admissibility or inadmissibility of which is dependent upon the existence or nonexistence of a preliminary fact.

PROMISSORY (NOTE) - A promise in writing to pay a specified sum at an expressed time, or on demand, or at sight, to a named person, or to his order, or bearer.

PROOF - The establishment by evidence of a requisite degree of belief concerning a fact in the mind of the trier of fact or the court.

PROPERTY - Includes both real and personal property.

PROPRIETARY (adj.) - Relating or pertaining to ownership; usually a single owner.

PROSECUTE - To carry on an action or other judicial proceeding; to proceed against a person criminally.

PROVISO - A limitation or condition in a legal instrument.

PROXIMATE - Immediate; nearest

PUBLIC EMPLOYEE - An officer, agent, or employee of a public entity.

PUBLIC ENTITY - Includes a national, state, county, city and county, city, district, public authority, public agency, or any other political subdivision or public corporation, whether foreign or domestic.

PUBLIC OFFICIAL - Includes an official of a political dubdivision of such state or territory and of a municipality.

PUNITIVE - Relating to punishment.

Q

QUASH - To make void.

QUASI - As if; as it were.

QUID PRO QUO - Something for something; the giving of one valuable thing for another.

QUITCLAIM (v.) - To release or relinquish claim or title to, especially in deeds to realty.

QUO WARRANTO - A legal procedure to test an official's right to a public office or the right to hold a franchise, or to hold an office in a domestic corporation.

R

RATIFY - To approve and sanction.

REAL PROPERTY - Includes lands, tenements, and hereditaments.

REALTY - A brief term for real property.

REBUT - To contradict; to refute, especially by evidence and arguments.

RECEIVER - A person who is appointed by the court to receive, and hold in trust property in litigation.

RECIDIVIST - Habitual criminal.

RECIPROCAL - Mutual.

RECOUPMENT - To keep back or get something which is due; also, it is the right of a defendant to have a deduction from the amount of the plaintiff's damages because the plaintiff has not fulfilled his part of the same contract.

RECROSS EXAMINATION - Examination of a witness by a cross-examiner subsequent to a redirect examination of the witness.

REDEEM - To release an estate or article from mortgage or pledge by paying the debt for which it stood as security.

REDIRECT EXAMINATION - Examination of a witness by the direct examiner subsequent to the cross-examination of the witness.

REFEREE - A person to whom a cause pending in a court is referred by the court, to take testimony, hear the parties, and report thereon to the court.

REFERENDUM - A method of submitting an important legislative or administrative matter to a direct vote of the people.

RELEVANT EVIDENCE - Evidence including evidence relevant to the credulity of a witness or hearsay declarant, having any tendency in reason to prove or disprove any disputed fact that is of consequence to the determination of the action.

REMAND - To send a case back to the lower court from which it came, for further proceedings.

REPLEVIN - An action to recover goods or chattels wrongfully taken or detained.

REPLY (REPLICATION) - Generally, a reply is what the plaintiff or other person who has instituted proceedings says in answer to the defendant's case.

RE JUDICATA - A thing judicially acted upon or decided.

RES ADJUDICATA - Doctrine that an issue or dispute litigated and determined in a case between the opposing parties is deemed permanently decided between these parties.

RESCIND (RECISSION) - To avoid or cancel a contract.

RESPONDENT - A defendant in a proceeding in chancery or admiralty; also, the person who contends against the appeal in a case.

RESTITUTION - In equity, it is the restoration of both parties to their original condition (when practicable), upon the rescission of a contract for fraud or similar cause.

RETROACTIVE (RETROSPECTIVE) - Looking back; effective as of a prior time.

REVERSED - A term used by appellate courts to indicate that the decision of the lower court in the case before it has been set aside.

REVOKE - To recall or cancel.

RIPARIAN (RIGHTS) - The rights of a person owning land containing or bordering on a water course or other body of water, such as lakes and rivers.

S

SALE - A contract whereby the ownership of property is transferred from one person to another for a sum of money or for any consideration.

SANCTION - A penalty or punishment provided as a means of enforcing obedience to a law; also, an authorization.

SATISFACTION - The discharge of an obligation by paying a party what is due to him; or what is awarded to him by the judgment of a court or otherwise.

SCIENTER - Knowingly; also, it is used in pleading to denote the defendant 's guilty knowledge.

SCINTILLA - A spark; also the least particle.

SECRET OF STATE - Governmental secret relating to the national defense or the international relations of the United States.

SECURITY - Indemnification; the term is applied to an obligation, such as a mortgage or deed of trust, given by a debtor to insure the payment or performance of his debt, by furnishing the creditor with a resource to be used in case of the debtor's failure to fulfill the principal obligation.

SENTENCE - The judgment formally pronounced by the court or judge upon the defendant after his conviction in a criminal prosecution.

SET-OFF - A claim or demand which one party in an action credits against the claim of the opposing party.

SHALL and MAY - "Shall" is mandatory and "may" is permissive.

SITUS - Location.

SOVEREIGN - A person, body or state in which independent and supreme authority is vested.

STARE DECISIS - To follow decided cases.

STATE - "State" means this State, unless applied to the different parts of the United States. In the latter case, it includes any state, district, commonwealth, territory or insular possession of the United States, including the District of Columbia.

STATEMENT - (a) Oral or written verbal expression or (b) nonverbal conduct of a person intended by him as a substitute for oral or written verbal expression.

STATUTE - An act of the legislature. Includes a treaty.

STATUTE OF LIMITATION - A statute limiting the time to bring an action after the right of action has arisen.

STAY - To hold in abeyance an order of a court.

STIPULATION - Any agreement made by opposing attorneys regulating any matter incidental to the proceedings or trial.

SUBORDINATION (AGREEMENT) - An agreement making one's rights inferior to or of a lower rank than another's.

SUBORNATION - The crime of procuring a person to lie or to make false statements to a court.

SUBPOENA - A writ or order directed to a person, and requiring his attendance at a particular time and place to testify as a witness.

SUBPOENA DUCES TECUM - A subpoena used, not only for the purpose of compelling witnesses to attend in court, but also requiring them to bring with them books or documents which may be in their possession, and which may tend to elucidate the subject matter of the trial.

SUBROGATION - The substituting of one for another as a creditor, the new creditor succeeding to the former's rights.

SUBSIDY - A government grant to assist a private enterprise deemed advantageous to the public.

SUI GENERIS - Of the same kind.

SUIT - Any civil proceeding by a person or persons against another or others in a court of justice by which the plaintiff pursues the remedies afforded him by law.

SUMMONS - A notice to a defendant that an action against him has been commenced and requiring him to appear in court and answer the complaint.

SUPRA - Above; this word occurring by itself in a book refers the reader to a previous part of the book.

SURETY - A person who binds himself for the payment of a sum of money, or for the performance of something else, for another.

SURPLUSAGE - Extraneous or unnecessary matter.

SURVIVORSHIP - A term used when a person becomes entitled to property by reason of his having survived another person who had an interest in the property.

SUSPEND SENTENCE - Hold back a sentence pending good behavior of prisoner.

SYLLABUS - A note prefixed to a report, especially a case, giving a brief statement of the court's ruling on different issues of the case.

T

TALESMAN - Person summoned to fill a panel of jurors.

TENANT - One who holds or possesses lands by any kind of right or title; also, one who has the temporary use and occupation of real property owned by another person (landlord), the duration and terms of his tenancy being usually fixed by an instrument called "a lease."

TENDER - An offer of money; an expression of willingness to perform a contract according to its terms.

TERM - When used with reference to a court, it signifies the period of time during which the court holds a session, usually of several weeks or months duration.

TESTAMENTARY - Pertaining to a will or the administration of a will.

TESTATOR (male)

TESTATRIX (female) - One who makes or has made a testament or will.

TESTIFY (TESTIMONY) - To give evidence under oath as a witness.

TO WIT - That is to say; namely.

TORT - Wrong; injury to the person.

TRANSITORY - Passing from place to place.

TRESPASS - Entry into another's ground, illegally.

TRIAL - The examination of a cause, civil or criminal, before a judge who has jurisdiction over it, according to the laws of the land.

TRIER OF FACT - Includes (a) the jury and (b) the court when the court is trying an issue of fact other than one relating to the admissibility of evidence.

TRUST - A right of property, real or personal, held by one party for the benefit of another.

TRUSTEE - One who lawfully holds property in custody for the benefit of another.

U

UNAVAILABLE AS A WITNESS - The declarant is (1) Exempted or precluded on the ground of privilege from testifying concerning the matter to which his statement is relevant; (2) Disqualified from testifying to the matter; (3) Dead or unable to attend or to testify at the hearing because of then existing physical or mental illness or infirmity; (4) Absent from the hearing and the court is unable to compel his attendance by its process; or (5) Absent from the hearing and the proponent of his statement has exercised reasonable diligence but has been unable to procure his attendance by the court's process.

ULTRA VIRES - Acts beyond the scope and power of a corporation, association, etc.

UNILATERAL - One-sided; obligation upon, or act of one party.

USURY - Unlawful interest on a loan.

V

VACATE - To set aside; to move out.

VARIANCE - A discrepancy or disagreement between two instruments or two aspects of the same case, which by law should be consistent.

VENDEE - A purchaser or buyer.

VENDOR - The person who transfers property by sale, particularly real estate; the term "seller" is used more commonly for one who sells personal property.

VENIREMEN - Persons ordered to appear to serve on a jury or composing a panel of jurors.

VENUE - The place at which an action is tried, generally based on locality or judicial district in which an injury occurred or a material fact happened.

VERDICT - The formal decision or finding of a jury.

VERIFY - To confirm or substantiate by oath.

VEST - To accrue to.

VOID - Having no legal force or binding effect.

VOIR DIRE - Preliminary examination of a witness or a juror to test competence, interest, prejudice, etc.

W

WAIVE - To give up a right.

WAIVER - The intentional or voluntary relinquishment of a known right.

WARRANT (WARRANTY) (v.) - To promise that a certain fact or state of facts, in relation to the subject matter, is, or shall be, as it is represented to be.

WARRANT (n.) - A writ issued by a judge, or other competent authority, addressed to a sheriff, or other officer, requiring him to arrest the person therein named, and bring him before the judge or court to answer or be examined regarding the offense with which he is charged.

WRIT - An order or process issued in the name of the sovereign or in the name of a court or judicial officer, commanding the performance or nonperformance of some act.

WRITING - Handwriting, typewriting, printing, photostating, photographing and every other means of recording upon any tangible thing any form of communication or representation, including letters, words, pictures, sounds, or symbols, or combinations thereof.

WRITINGS AND RECORDINGS - Consists of letters, words, or numbers, or their equivalent, set down by handwriting, typewriting, printing, photostating, photographing, magnetic impulse, mechanical or electronic recording, or other form of data compilation.

Y

YEA AND NAY - Yes and no.

YELLOW DOG CONTRACT - A contract by which employer requires employee to sign an instrument promising as condition that he will not join a union during its continuance, and will be discharged if he does join.

Z

ZONING - The division of a city by legislative regulation into districts and the prescription and application in each district of regulations having to do with structural and architectural designs of buildings and of regulations prescribing use to which buildings within designated districts may be put.

ANSWER SHEET

NO. ______________ PART ________ TITLE OF POSITION ______________________________
(AS GIVEN IN EXAMINATION ANNOUNCEMENT - INCLUDE OPTION, IF ANY)

OF EXAMINATION ______________________________ ______________________________ DATE ____________
(CITY OR TOWN) (STATE)

RATING

USE THE SPECIAL PENCIL. MAKE GLOSSY BLACK MARKS.

A B C D E	A B C D E	A B C D E	A B C D E	A B C D E
1	26	51	76	101
2	27	52	77	102
3	28	53	78	103
4	29	54	79	104
5	30	55	80	105
6	31	56	81	106
7	32	57	82	107
8	33	58	83	108
9	34	59	84	109
10	35	60	85	110

Make only ONE mark for each answer. Additional and stray marks may be counted as mistakes. In making corrections, erase errors COMPLETELY.

A B C D E	A B C D E	A B C D E	A B C D E	A B C D E
11	36	61	86	111
12	37	62	87	112
13	38	63	88	113
14	39	64	89	114
15	40	65	90	115
16	41	66	91	116
17	42	67	92	117
18	43	68	93	118
19	44	69	94	119
20	45	70	95	120
21	46	71	96	121
22	47	72	97	122
23	48	73	98	123
24	49	74	99	124
25	50	75	100	125

ANSWER SHEET

TEST NO. _____ PART _____ TITLE OF POSITION _____
(AS GIVEN IN EXAMINATION ANNOUNCEMENT - INCLUDE OPTION, IF ANY)

PLACE OF EXAMINATION _____ DATE _____
(CITY OR TOWN)   (STATE)

RATING

USE THE SPECIAL PENCIL.   MAKE GLOSSY BLACK MARKS.

	A B C D E		A B C D E		A B C D E		A B C D E		A B C D
1	:: :: :: :: ::	26	:: :: :: :: ::	51	:: :: :: :: ::	76	:: :: :: :: ::	101	:: :: :: ::
2	:: :: :: :: ::	27	:: :: :: :: ::	52	:: :: :: :: ::	77	:: :: :: :: ::	102	:: :: :: ::
3	:: :: :: :: ::	28	:: :: :: :: ::	53	:: :: :: :: ::	78	:: :: :: :: ::	103	:: :: :: ::
4	:: :: :: :: ::	29	:: :: :: :: ::	54	:: :: :: :: ::	79	:: :: :: :: ::	104	:: :: :: ::
5	:: :: :: :: ::	30	:: :: :: :: ::	55	:: :: :: :: ::	80	:: :: :: :: ::	105	:: :: :: ::
6	:: :: :: :: ::	31	:: :: :: :: ::	56	:: :: :: :: ::	81	:: :: :: :: ::	106	:: :: :: ::
7	:: :: :: :: ::	32	:: :: :: :: ::	57	:: :: :: :: ::	82	:: :: :: :: ::	107	:: :: :: ::
8	:: :: :: :: ::	33	:: :: :: :: ::	58	:: :: :: :: ::	83	:: :: :: :: ::	108	:: :: :: ::
9	:: :: :: :: ::	34	:: :: :: :: ::	59	:: :: :: :: ::	84	:: :: :: :: ::	109	:: :: :: ::
10	:: :: :: :: ::	35	:: :: :: :: ::	60	:: :: :: :: ::	85	:: :: :: :: ::	110	:: :: :: ::

Make only ONE mark for each answer.   Additional and stray marks may be
counted as mistakes.   In making corrections, erase errors COMPLETELY.

	A B C D E		A B C D E		A B C D E		A B C D E		A B C D
11	:: :: :: :: ::	36	:: :: :: :: ::	61	:: :: :: :: ::	86	:: :: :: :: ::	111	:: :: :: ::
12	:: :: :: :: ::	37	:: :: :: :: ::	62	:: :: :: :: ::	87	:: :: :: :: ::	112	:: :: :: ::
13	:: :: :: :: ::	38	:: :: :: :: ::	63	:: :: :: :: ::	88	:: :: :: :: ::	113	:: :: :: ::
14	:: :: :: :: ::	39	:: :: :: :: ::	64	:: :: :: :: ::	89	:: :: :: :: ::	114	:: :: :: ::
15	:: :: :: :: ::	40	:: :: :: :: ::	65	:: :: :: :: ::	90	:: :: :: :: ::	115	:: :: :: ::
16	:: :: :: :: ::	41	:: :: :: :: ::	66	:: :: :: :: ::	91	:: :: :: :: ::	116	:: :: :: ::
17	:: :: :: :: ::	42	:: :: :: :: ::	67	:: :: :: :: ::	92	:: :: :: :: ::	117	:: :: :: ::
18	:: :: :: :: ::	43	:: :: :: :: ::	68	:: :: :: :: ::	93	:: :: :: :: ::	118	:: :: :: ::
19	:: :: :: :: ::	44	:: :: :: :: ::	69	:: :: :: :: ::	94	:: :: :: :: ::	119	:: :: :: ::
20	:: :: :: :: ::	45	:: :: :: :: ::	70	:: :: :: :: ::	95	:: :: :: :: ::	120	:: :: :: ::
21	:: :: :: :: ::	46	:: :: :: :: ::	71	:: :: :: :: ::	96	:: :: :: :: ::	121	:: :: :: ::
22	:: :: :: :: ::	47	:: :: :: :: ::	72	:: :: :: :: ::	97	:: :: :: :: ::	122	:: :: :: ::
23	:: :: :: :: ::	48	:: :: :: :: ::	73	:: :: :: :: ::	98	:: :: :: :: ::	123	:: :: :: ::
24	:: :: :: :: ::	49	:: :: :: :: ::	74	:: :: :: :: ::	99	:: :: :: :: ::	124	:: :: :: ::
25	:: :: :: :: ::	50	:: :: :: :: ::	75	:: :: :: :: ::	100	:: :: :: :: ::	125	:: :: :: ::